THE SIGN OF LOVE

The Sign of Love

REFLECTIONS ON
THE EUCHARIST

Timothy Gorringe

SPCK

TISEC

First published in Great Britain in 1997
Society for Promoting Christian Knowledge
Holy Trinity Church
Marylebone Road
London NW1 4DU

British Library Cataloguing-in-Publication Data
A catalogue record of this book is available from
the British Library

ISBN 0-281-04996-3

Typeset by Wilmaset Ltd, Birkenhead, Wirral
Printed in Great Britain by
Biddles Ltd, Guildford and King's Lynn

To M, H and I
Disturbers of the eucharistic peace

CONTENTS

1

Signs of Hope

A LITTLE OVER seventy years after the crucifixion of Jesus we begin to find a great deal of confusion and suspicion amongst non-Christians over certain Christian practices. In a famous letter probably written in 109 AD, the younger Pliny reports to the Emperor Trajan that he has pulled in a large number of people for questioning in response to an anonymous pamphlet accusing people of being Christians. He learned from interviewing these people that Christians met regularly before dawn on a fixed day to sing hymns to Christ 'as to a God', to bind themselves to do nothing immoral and then 'to take food of an ordinary, harmless kind'. With a chilling logic only too familiar to the police chiefs and local army commanders of the present century he decided that, since he had found nothing untoward, he had better extract 'the truth' by torture from two deaconesses. 'I found nothing but a degenerate sort of cult carried to extravagant lengths.'[1]

We do not learn what happened to the two deaconesses. Did they recover from their torture, or did they, like Origen a hundred and fifty years later, die slowly and painfully as a result of the injuries they received? Did they confront their torturers, like the heroine in Ariel Dorfman's *Death and the Maiden*? There is no one to tell their story. We know them only because they appear in the margins of a governor's report, as today we know of tens of thousands of 'disappeared' who find their way into the Amnesty statistics.

Eighty years after this incident, in North Africa, the

Christian apologist Tertullian notes that 'We are accused of observing a holy rite in which we kill a little child and then eat it, and at the end of our banquet revel in incest.'[2] This kind of rumour seems to have been quite common, and obviously has its roots in the language about 'body and blood' which stood at the heart of Christian eucharistic practice.

Right at the beginning of the Christian story, perhaps in 55 AD, Paul takes it for granted that Christians will gather for 'the supper of the Lord' (1 Corinthians 11.20), and he sets out the practice in terms of the tradition he received. This tradition now constitutes the heart of our own eucharistic liturgy:

> I received from the Lord what I also handed on to you, that the Lord Jesus on the night when he was betrayed took a loaf of bread, and when he had given thanks, he broke it and said, 'This is my body that is for you. Do this in remembrance of me.' In the same way he took the cup also, after supper, saying, 'This cup is the new covenant in my blood. Do this as often as you drink it, in remembrance of me.' (1 Corinthians 11.23–5)

It seems probable from the prominence this narrative has in the Synoptic Gospels, and the way it is reflected on in the sixth chapter of John's Gospel, that the eucharist stood from the beginning at the centre of Christian life together. This is confirmed by writers throughout the second and third centuries. Thus the writer of the *Didache*, which may date from the last years of the first century, tells his readers: 'Assemble on the Lord's Day, and break bread and offer the Eucharist.' Ignatius of Antioch, on his way to martyrdom in Rome, writes: 'Take care to keep Eucharist', and to another church, 'Be eager for more frequent gatherings for thanksgiving (eucharist) to God and for his glory. For when you meet frequently the forces of Satan are annulled.'[3] In the middle of the second century another apologist, Justin, explains Christian practice to the educated Roman public telling how 'On that day which is called after the sun all who are in the towns and in the country gather together for a communal celebration.' His picture of what happens is very beautiful. First the writings of apostles and prophets are read, 'as long as time permits'; then follows an exhortation by the president,

> Then we all rise together and pray and, when our prayer is ended, bread and wine and water are brought, and the president in like manner offers prayers and thanksgivings, according to his ability, and the people assent, saying Amen; and there is a distribution to each, and a participation of that over which thanks have been given, and to those who are absent a portion is sent by the deacons. And they who are well to do, and willing, give what each thinks fit; and what is collected is deposited with the president, who succours the orphans and widows, and those who, through sickness or any other cause, are in want, and those who are in bonds, and the strangers sojourning among us, and in a word takes care of all who are in need. But Sunday is the day on which we all hold our common assembly, because it is the first day on which God, having wrought a change in the darkness and matter, made the world; and Jesus Christ our Saviour on the same day rose from the dead.[4]

So it goes on. Writer after writer testifies to the centrality of the eucharist in Christian common life. Why was it, when contemporary society found the practice alien and suspicious, that the eucharist remained so important? Why has that continued to be true over nearly two thousand years

3

through a whole variety of understandings of what the eucharist means? Is it still true for us? We are no longer accused of cannibalism and incest, but deep-rooted suspicions of other kinds remain. I was taken aback when, after a beautiful eucharist in a tiny medieval chapel near Oxford, a place where without question 'prayer has been valid', a student who had attended but not come up to receive communion burst out: 'It's all so much mumbo-jumbo! All that stuff about transubstantiation! I can't understand how intelligent people go on with it.' This kind of objection to sacramental practice is more widespread than those of us who think of the sacraments as essential to our living and breathing realize.

What I hope to show is that the eucharist has been central to Christian common life because of the way in which it intersects with our daily life – the whole fabric of our social, political and economic reality. In a unique way it bathes that daily reality in the light of the Triune God, teaching us that our lives and our world are gifts. They are not something to hoard, corner or crow over – as if what we have or can do are the results of our own efforts – but are for us to share as the response to love. 'Freely [you] have received: freely give' (Matthew 10.8 AV). This teaching of Jesus is what is signified in the eucharist. The eucharist is a sign of God's reality amongst us, at the depths of our world, and therefore a sign of the connectedness of daily reality to God. As such it is a sign of hope in a world where that commodity is often enough hard to come by. To understand the eucharist, then, we need to have some understanding of the importance of signs.

Humans are sign-giving creatures. This is as much a definition of what we are as to say that we are rational creatures (*homo sapiens*) or creatures which play (*homo ludens*). Signs are our means of communication, at all sorts of levels. The most fundamental signs, which constitute the framework of our common life, are words. Words are conventions which enable us to recognize and respond to the world. I say 'tree'; she says, '*l'arbre*'; he says '*der Baum*'. All of us point to one reality, naming according to a local convention. Scripts are signs, which we must learn to decipher: watch young children as they learn to read, puzzling over the signs, learning to make connections between these signs and reality (often through pictures: t-r-e-e – picture of tree – tree in the garden). Words may indeed have originated as hieroglyphs or pictograms.

Fundamental as they are in the universe of signs, there has nevertheless always been a certain distrust of words. 'Words are what we use when we have sod all to say', says the Australian songwriter Eric Bogle, and people have always sought to go beyond words, to clothe words in flesh, by signifying through flowers, rings, gifts and monuments. Amongst the most mysterious of all signs is musical notation, a mystery which suggested to Plato a whole theory of the universe. Some philosophers have thought of the universe as a 'book of signs', and the argument to the existence and nature of God from the beauty and design of the universe makes something like this assumption. In that case absolutely everything can be a sign, and there is a sense in which this is evidently true for the Christian: existence is God's basic gift and creation the product of God's love. It is a sign, or a set of signs, which it is our daily task to construe. We have already noted a sufficient wealth of signs, however, to show that we must learn to distinguish, for there are signs and signs.

Consider, for example, the story in Jorge Semprun's remarkable book, *Oh, What a Beautiful Sunday!*. Semprun was a communist who was interned in one of the Nazi death camps, near Weimar. Aryan prisoners in these camps were used for work in munitions factories, and his book begins with, and continually comes back to, an encounter with a tree he had one Sunday, returning from an unscheduled visit to the factory. Returning alone he was suddenly caught by the beauty of a single snow-encrusted birch. In that tree the beauty and mystery of the universe suddenly became radiant and transparent. He left the path and went up to it, scraping the snow off the bark. Suddenly a challenge: 'What do you think you're doing?' The click of the safety catch of a revolver being released, and a member of the SS coming menacingly towards him. Death was the penalty for trying to escape, and he had left the path ... All he could say was, 'The tree ... It's so beautiful.' In the midst of the worst form of human evil the world suddenly became transparent with glory, luminous. 'Things' become signs. It is possible to say 'Thou' to a tree, said Martin Buber, but in fact all sorts of realities, from Moses' bush irradiated by sunlight to Semprun's snow-covered birch, can suddenly leap from the taken-for-granted background and become signs.

Signs play a considerable part in the biblical narrative. According to the authors of Genesis 9, the rainbow is a sign. Coming as it does at the end of a storm it becomes a sign of the positive transcending the negative, of God's benevolence experienced in the regularity of nature. This idea could be generalized to the whole of creation. 'The heavens declare the glory of God', said the psalmist. Paul picked up this line of thinking in his letter to the Romans: God's 'eternal power and divine nature, invisible though they are, have been understood and seen through the things he has made' (Romans 1.20). The whole created order becomes as it were a sign of God's love and constancy.

The phrase 'signs and wonders' crops up frequently in the Hebrew Bible where it refers above all to the plagues which compelled Pharaoh to release Israel from Egypt. Other miraculous signs are associated with Gideon, Elijah and Elisha. All these signs are manifestations of God's power to save and heal in response to the cry of God's people. A sign here is something unusual and out of the ordinary, quite different from the sign-fabric of our lives that words represent.

The prophets of Israel often gave their contemporaries 'signs' in a very different sense. These were odd, striking, but decidedly not miraculous events. Isaiah, for example, wrote the words 'Spoil speeds, prey hastens' on a tile before witnesses and gave this name to his unfortunate child as a sign of what God would do through the Assyrians (Isaiah 8.3f.). Jeremiah bought a new loincloth (not Y-fronts but more like the contemporary Indian dhoti), wore it without bothering to shrink it, and then hid it in rocks until it rotted as a sign of what was going to happen to Judah (Jeremiah 13.4f.). Ezekiel drew a picture of Jerusalem besieged on a clay brick and lay facing the brick with an iron plate between him and the brick as a sign of the same thing (Ezekiel 4.1f.). These signs were supposed to be effective and to hasten the events they signified. Before we write them off as sympathetic magic perhaps we should reflect on the impact they might have had in the small communities of their day. A contemporary example might be the self-immolation of Jan Palach in Prague in 1968 after the Russian invasion. Who can say that this terrible tragic protest did nothing towards the eventual withdrawal and crumbling of that regime? Signs like this have the capacity to go deeper than acres of newspaper comment.

Jesus spoke a good deal about signs. It seems he was often asked to provide a 'sign', in the sense of a striking and miraculous occurrence, which would remove all ambiguity about his person. He rejected this demand as a temptation and said that 'no sign shall be given except the sign of Jonah' (Matthew 12.39). Presumably the point here is that Jonah did no sign, but only *preached* to the people of Nineveh. Jesus also warned that false prophets would work signs (Matthew 24.24). At the same time he implied that people should be able to 'read the signs of the times' and when the messengers of John the Baptist came to ask him, 'Are you the one who is to come?' Jesus referred them to the messianic signs mentioned by Isaiah:

> Go and tell John what you hear and see: the blind receive their sight, the lame walk, the lepers are cleansed, the deaf hear, the dead are raised, and the poor have good news brought to them. (Matthew 11.4 cf. Isaiah 35.5–6)

For centuries, Jesus' miracles were taken to be 'proofs' of his divinity, but his rejection of the demand for signs ought to put us on our guard about such a reading. In the passage from Isaiah to which Jesus refers the point is to take courage from the promises of God. Jesus is saying that the messianic age has indeed arrived, but he insists at the same time that 'wonders' are not the proof of that. The focus of the gospel miracles is not spectacular demonstrations of power, represented as a demonic temptation in the story of Jesus' testing by the devil, but the fact that people are healed and restored to the community. This, at any rate, seems to be the way the evangelist John understands Jesus' miracles. He uses the word 'sign' to refer to them, and tells us that he records them so that people may have faith that Jesus is the Christ, the Son of God (John 20.30f.). On the other hand the signs do not in any sense compel faith but on the contrary generate controversy and are often met with unbelief (John 12.37).

That signs may be met with unbelief precisely shows

their mediating status. They are not the thing itself, but they point beyond themselves. When we are dealing with God we need signs because 'No one shall see [God] and live' (Exodus 33.20). There is simply no way we can have God's reality as it were at first hand. We need signs both to make present to us the God who is not a member of this universe, and to protect us.

The fact that we live by signs has always exercised a great fascination for philosophers. Perhaps the whole of reality is but a sign world? One can understand the fascination, but on the other hand the distinction between signs and reality remains important. The word 'food' does not fill my stomach and help me grow. Real food does. This is where talk about 'mere signs' comes from.

The question of whether we have a 'real' presence in the eucharist or whether it is a 'mere' sign generated vast quantities of hot air in the sixteenth century. At a famous meeting between Luther and Zwingli, Luther hit the table and insisted that the eucharistic elements were not 'mere signs' but truly Christ's body and blood. No one sought to point out that the difference between the two Reformers was not over the eucharist but over the nature of the real. Zwingli was working with Platonic ideas for which signs might be the 'really real'. Luther, who walked to work each day through a farmyard, and who had a practical peasant's sense of what was real and what was not, insisted that 'This *is* my body' must mean that a change in the eucharistic elements took place.

In this century, this debate has been taken further precisely in terms of an understanding of the nature of signs. What we have in the eucharist, it is argued, is not transubstantiation – a view which in any case needed the metaphysics of Aristotle to make it stick – but *trans-signification*. We take bread and wine – the stuff of ordinary life, symbols of basic nourishment and of celebration – and we place them in quite a different context, within the context of the story of God's redeeming activity. In this case what they signify is changed. This does not mean a change at the level of subatomic particles. It does mean that at the level of signifying, at the level of the social world which human beings occupy, the bread and wine are quite different. In attempting to spell out what the social, economic and political significance of the eucharist is, then, I am trying to show how the bread and wine of the eucharist is trans-signified. Luther was expressing the prejudice of the 'plain man' in insisting that unless there was a substantial change there was no change at all. Taking Zwingli's side is to invite misunderstanding, but we have to say he had the best of the argument, being open to see that our interpretation of reality is, in fact, part of that reality.

The word which has traditionally been used to designate the sign character of the eucharist is 'sacrament'. So the Heidelberg Catechism defined sacraments as 'visible, holy signs and seals instituted by God in order that by their use he may the more fully disclose and seal to us the promise of the gospel'. The route by which the word 'sacrament' came to mean 'sacred sign' is very obscure. In classical Latin a *sacramentum* was a legal bond, or bail or the military oath of allegiance. From thence it came to mean a solemn oath, or engagement. This latter use suggested its use to describe baptism. At the beginning of the fifth century, Augustine tells us that 'Signs which pertain to divine things are called sacraments.'[5] When he is discussing sacrifice he says: 'A sacrifice is the visible sacrament or sacred sign of an invisible sacrifice.' The sacrifice he has in mind is a moral one: 'The sacrifice the Church celebrates in the sacrament of the altar ... where it is shown to her that in this thing which she offers she herself is offered.'[6] From this discussion came the classic Western definition of a sacrament as 'an outward and visible sign of an inward and spiritual grace'.

Augustine did not limit the word 'sacrament' to liturgical actions of the Church such as baptism and eucharist. For him the word had a much broader reference. Through the centuries the meaning got steadily narrower. By the early Middle Ages, people were proposing that there were perhaps thirty sacraments. Peter Lombard, Archbishop of Paris in 1150, restricted the number to seven. In this he was followed by Aquinas and then by the Council of Trent in the sixteenth century, which spoke of 'seven sacraments, no more and no less'. These were eucharist, baptism, confirmation, ordination, marriage, penance and extreme unction. By this time the word 'sacrament' refers only to liturgical acts of the Church.

Luther debated whether to return to the New Testament use and speak of Christ as the only true sign of God's love. Later he fixed on 'baptism and bread' as being the only two sacraments of the Church, being the only two promises 'with signs attached'. In this he was followed by all the Reformed Churches. On the extreme left wing of the Reformation, however, there were groups which felt this did not go far enough. For them the word alone was all that was needed. This group was represented by the Quakers at the end of the seventeenth century and, at the end of the nineteenth century, by the Salvation Army.

Throughout the twentieth century there has been a progressive reopening of the concept. The Scottish theologian John Oman believed that life itself was 'the one Supreme Divine Sacrament' and the sacraments of the Church exist 'to express and, as it were, give the concentrated essence of the sacrament of life'.[7] All forms of human sharing and expressions of compassion, tenderness or love are, for Oman, sacraments. Many of those who took this up like to speak of a 'sacramental universe' or the 'sacramental principle'.

In the Roman Catholic Church, since the Second Vatican Council, a popular view has been to think in terms of a hierarchy of sacraments. Christ is the 'arch sacrament'; the Church is the 'fundamental sacrament' (sign of a sign) and the eucharist and other church sacraments are in turn signs of this. Christ is the basic sign of God's love to the world. The Church exists to speak about the incarnation of this love, and the sacraments are one form of this speech.

In a beautiful essay written in 1970 the Catholic theologian Karl Rahner went further than this.[8] The problem with Oman's theology of the 'sacramental universe' was that it easily suggested a kind of pantheism. Notoriously pantheism finds it difficult to say a clear-cut 'No' to evil. Rahner transforms this by speaking of history, rather than of creation, as God's liturgy. Creation is the product of 'grace', God's will to share Godself. When creation becomes history in the emergence of human beings, who become subjects of their own history, history remains imbued with grace. Rahner thinks of human history as a vast liturgy, celebrated both in joy and sorrow, depth and superficiality, love and hatred. The crucifixion puts Christ at the heart of this whole liturgy. What the Church sacraments do is to reflect upon the liturgy and make known the fact that God is to be found in it, even in all its folly and wickedness. Unless this connection is made at the deepest level the Church sacraments become 'empty ritual attitudinizings, full of unbelief'. The eucharist is celebrated in the knowledge that the world already offers itself in 'rejoicing, tears and blood'. The Church sacraments then are signs of 'grace' – the openness and fundamental hopefulness of human history under God's pedagogy.

Humans are sign-giving creatures. Beyond the very basic forms of sign-giving (for instance, to signal that you need water in an area where you do not know the language) this capacity for making signs has enabled people to explore the heights and depths of the universe conceptually, visually, geometrically and musically. Poetry, philosophy, music, physics and chemistry – all this is a sign world the function of which is to explore and celebrate the mystery of the given. Liturgy is part of this aspect of the sign world. It has its own reality, which must be respected – reality as signifying. When it is mistaken for essential reality it is fetishized. The 'true bread' of the eucharist is no substitute for the bread which feeds the hungry. It is true bread, the bread of life, only when it leads us to feed the hungry. But it is also, like philosophy and art, a way of exploring the depths of our world. Unlike poetry or philosophy it is not the result primarily of human reflection on the mystery of creation. Rather, it is a response to a given, to the heart of the mystery making itself known, to what theologians call 'revelation'. It is a re-presentation of the heart of the divine self-giving to history. The point of re-presentation is that the divine story shapes our story, and is able to take on new creative dimensions through us.

Talk of the way in which the story shapes us leads to an important distinction between symbols and signs. Paul Tillich defined a symbol thus:

> Symbols . . . are intrinsically related to what they express; they have inherent qualities (water, fire, oil, bread, wine) which make them adequate to their symbolic function . . . A sacramental symbol is neither a thing nor a sign. It participates in the power of what it symbolizes, and therefore it can be the medium of the Spirit.[9]

Sacraments *use* symbols, but they are not themselves symbols, but signs. Tillich's definition makes clear that symbols relate to the order of creation. A sign relates more to the order of redemption. The difference between the two is that the latter involves a story, it locates us within redemption history. The former expresses, by contrast, something of the beauty and power of creation.

Whether it is the fact that something 'participates in the power of what it symbolizes' which makes it a medium of the Spirit is very much open to question. It is true that the eucharist, like every cultic act, uses symbols: light in the form of candles, bread and wine which signify the satisfaction of need and celebration. The inexhaustible depth of meaning in the eucharist gains from this symbolic function. The use of vestments, altar hangings, liturgical colours, all appeal to the 'forest of symbols'.

On the other hand, the tradition of Israel seems from the start to have been wary of symbols. Their introduction of symbols into the Jerusalem Temple was the result of the need to assimilate the Jebusite cult and to come to terms with the culture of Canaan. For good or ill this symbolic tradition was never domesticated in Israel. Myth, said the Old Testament scholar von Rad, is a way of thinking by means of symbols and images, and Israel fought against the capacity of mythic symbols to serve as means of revelation with all her might. 'This awareness of the barrier which men erect between themselves and God by means of images is ... Israel's greatest achievement.'[10]

Von Rad worked in Heidelberg, and in his lifetime had seen the erection of the neo-pagan Tingstatte, a sort of amphitheatre, in the woods above the city. Goebbels had it built as a focus for Nazi rallies glorifying the 'Aryan' past. Von Rad therefore had every reason to be aware of the way symbols and images could be used in the service of a demonic mythicization. Symbols are ambiguous. All of the great symbols can be used within both divine and demonic cults.

Though the Temple was full of symbols Israel's liturgy centred around narrative, and it is at least suggestive that when the Temple was destroyed Israel survived without any sign of trauma.

Signs as opposed to symbols have a particular story attached to them: the use of bitter herbs at the Passover to signify the suffering of slavery, for example; the use of bread and wine in the eucharist to recall Jesus' last meal with his disciples. The great event of salvation, the exodus from Egypt, was recalled in the Passover liturgy. 'Let everyone live as if they came forth out of Egypt' said a Passover rubric and it is the liturgy which made this possible. The point of the eucharist is, like the Passover, to offer us a clue to what God is up to in human history. The sign-giving does not aim to take us back to the first century; the eucharist is not a time machine. Rather, it catches us into the stream of God's continuing and liberating activity. It goes without saying that only the signs, rather than the symbols, can do this. The signs speak of a God who is humiliated, cursed and spat upon. They take us into the heart of the darkness of the gospel, the folly which is wisdom and the wisdom which is folly, the weakness which is strength and the strength which is weakness. No symbol rooted in the order of creation could do this. The symbols speak to us of God's love but do not lead us into the mystery of redemption. They are ambiguous about the threat to creation by death, disease, wickedness. The signs take us to the heart of that darkness and illuminate it with the light of redemption. They are signs of hope. How we are to understand that is the theme of the following reflections.

2

The Open Table

WHEN PAUL RECALLS the significance of the eucharist for his Corinthian hearers he does so by rehearsing the tradition of the 'Last Supper', as we saw in the previous chapter. Paul scarcely ever appeals directly to the gospel narrative and it seems clear that by the early fifties of the first century this story was already a central part of the Church's liturgy, as it has remained ever since. This fact suggested to later theologians that what we have here is the account of the 'institution' of the eucharist. The command to 'do this in remembrance of me' was taken to refer to a set of liturgical actions – take, break, share. I wish to question both whether we can understand the command to 'do this' in terms of a ritual, and also to argue that our understanding of the eucharist is damagingly constricted unless we set it against a much wider background in the practice of Jesus than simply his last meal with his disciples.

Did Jesus intend to institute a ritual, on the night before his death? We cannot say this is impossible, but on the other hand it is not wholly consistent with what else we know about Jesus. According to Matthew he twice cites Hosea 6.6: 'I desire mercy, and not sacrifice', and reiterates over and over again in that Gospel that it is in 'doing' that discipleship consists and not in the 'Lord, Lord' of pious worship. Jesus clearly did not despise the practice of either synagogue or Temple, but ritual practice is equally clearly not at the forefront of the training of his disciples. In the great humorous parable of the sheep and the goats nothing is said about ritual or religious practice narrowly defined.

What counts, in the final reckoning, is feeding the hungry, showing hospitality to the stranger, clothing the poor, visiting the sick and those in prison – all the traditional virtues of Israel. This is the significant 'doing' at the heart of Jesus' teaching, and it seems more plausible to read the command to 'do this' in the light of that. To take this further we need first to turn to the question of Jesus' 'doing' in the Gospels, and especially to his table fellowship.

That table fellowship was an extremely important matter to Jesus is one of the best attested facts of the New Testament. From his critics we hear the angry question: 'Why does he eat with tax-collectors and sinners?'(Mark 2.16). In other words, if he is really setting himself up as some kind of authority, what is he doing eating with people who collaborate with the Romans and make themselves rich at the expense of decent, serious, religious citizens? What is he doing eating with people who disregard strict observance of the law? The fact that, as Jesus put it, 'The Son of Man has come eating and drinking' led to the jibe that Jesus was nothing but 'a glutton and a drunkard' (Luke 7.34; Matthew 11.19).

We have many stories in all our sources, but especially in Luke, of Jesus 'at table'. Luke puts the criticism of the scribes in the context of a meal at the house of Levi (Luke 5.29f.). He tells of a meal with a Pharisee where the proper rites of welcome were omitted by the host and performed by 'a woman ... who was a sinner' (Luke 7.36f.). Jesus tells many parables about wedding feasts, great banquets and celebration meals which were sacraments of reconciliation, and the damnation incurred by the meals of the rich whilst the poor starve (Luke 14.7f., 12f., 15f.; 15.22f.; 16.19f.). Jesus is not interested in food for its own sake: 'Don't be anxious about what you are going to eat and drink', he tells those who come to hear him; the kingdom is more important than that. But he never neglects material needs either: 'Give her something to eat', he tells the ruler of the synagogue and his wife, after healing their daughter (Mark 5.43). Table fellowship is for him, as it is for the society of his day in general, a sign of acceptance and close friendship. Precisely for this reason his opponents are shocked by the bad company he keeps at table. In Jesus' hands table fellowship is not about having a nice evening with those you like, having a dinner party. It becomes an instrument in his purpose of making people whole. The story which illustrates this in a paradigmatic way is that of Zacchaeus (Luke 19.1–10).

The story comes, in Luke, after we have heard about the rich man and Lazarus, and after Jesus' warning of the difficulty the rich will have in entering the kingdom of God. Camels could get through eyes of needles more easily says Jesus, in a typical jest. Zacchaeus is a man who has camelized himself for years – making a fortune by extorting taxes. He is not just an outcast but a rich outcast. Jesus restores his humanity, 'de-camelizes' him, redeems him by – inviting himself to dinner! It is the fact that Jesus shares table fellowship with him which leads Zacchaeus to change his lifestyle, to live no longer for Mammon, to restore what he has extorted, with interest. This restoration of a person's humanity, this drawing out of human potential, is what Jesus has come for, and table fellowship is one of the chosen ways of accomplishing it. The New Testament scholar Joachim Jeremias spoke of Jesus' parables as 'weapons of war', and similarly the exorcisms and healing stories depict Jesus at war with 'the powers'. But table fellowship is also part of Jesus' armoury, part of the whole structure of redemption.

Why should we think that these stories of table fellowship have anything to do with the eucharist? I think we have a clue in Luke's great story of the walk to Emmaus, where Jesus is known to the disciples 'in the breaking of bread'. The significance of this is that it is a characteristic action, a habit or custom, which reveals Jesus' identity. What Jesus did at the 'last' supper was to repeat something he did all the time, namely, invest table fellowship with tremendous significance. My suggestion is, then, that Jesus acted as he did at his last meal with his disciples because from the beginning he had used table fellowship redemptively. No one doubts this. The problem is that the connection with the eucharist has not been made because a reading of the Last Supper in terms of vicarious sacrifice has stood in the way. I do not wish to deny that this may be part of the truth, but I cannot believe it is the whole of it.

To take this a little further I turn to John's Gospel. This Gospel, it seems to me, is our earliest commentary on Mark. I am not claiming that John had a text of Mark in front of him, but John's text seems to originate in a long and rich exposition, probably over many years, of the material of the Synoptic Gospels, especially in their starkest form, in Mark. In his great Prologue, John speaks of Jesus as being 'full of grace and truth'. What he means by 'grace' here is exemplified by Jesus' practice of table fellowship. Jesus is 'full of grace' in that he does not hedge the possibility of friendship with moral ifs and buts. He does not say to Zacchaeus: 'If you will guarantee to return to the poor all you took I will come to eat with you.' He invites himself to dinner, restores Zacchaeus' self-worth and self-esteem, and *thus enables* repentance. Grace is, in the technical term, prevenient – it does not follow after, but anticipates. Like the shepherd in Jesus' parables it seeks out the lost, and does not wait for them first of all to come back to the fold. An immense amount has been lost by not understanding the 'grace' of the eucharistic table in these terms; that is, of an open, accepting, forgiving fellowship. 'Grace is forgiveness', Luther used to say. That was exemplified by Jesus' eating with bad company, which was not connivance with evil, but a way of shaming, humbling and converting it, by love and not by force. At issue is what we understand to be the reality of grace. Cardinal Newman sought a 'higher gift than grace' to refine flesh and blood. This was

> God's presence and his very self
> and essence all divine.

The grace which was 'channelled' by the sacraments was thought of as a kind of divine energy which enabled us to live the Christian life. In an attempt to understand how it was that not all baptized Christians led lives worthy of their calling all sorts of distinctions between 'sufficient' and 'efficient', habitual and actual, created and uncreated grace were introduced. Though these distinctions often arose out of wrestling with real problems, many theologians have recognized that we need to go back to our origins and learn afresh why the word *charis*, translated as 'grace', was so important to Paul.

In both Old and New Testament studies, scholars have countered the apologetic insistence on the difference of both Israel and Jesus from their contemporary cultures by showing how much they shared. The word *charis*, however, seems to be one of those irreducibly angular features which cannot be explained out of its environment. Paul takes a word which means beauty, thankfulness, delight, kindness, and uses it as a pen portrait of Jesus. Why? Because, surely, these attributes capture Jesus' encounter with others, and especially with 'sinners' and the poor. Grace is God's love reaching out to us absolutely irrespective of our worthiness, restoring us, making us more human, by acceptance and forgiveness and not by acting as a High Court judge. This is the essence of the doctrine of justification which was so important to Luther. Grace is not 'a' power, nor could we possibly want a 'higher gift than grace'. The word 'grace' is a way of talking about how God approaches us, specifically about how God approaches us in Christ. Grace is mediated to us in and through encounter, both in the Church and outside it. It is an exact description of the quality of the meeting between Jesus and Zacchaeus, a meeting imaged in the encounter between the Risen Lord and the Church in the eucharist.

If the eucharist is, then, rooted in Jesus' table fellowship with sinners, not exclusively, but as importantly as it is rooted in the Last Supper, what an irony it is that receiving communion was hedged about in the way it was with dire warnings to 'the wicked'. If we eat and drink unworthily, according to the homilies in the Book of Common Prayer, 'We eat and drink our own damnation . . . we kindle God's wrath against us; we provoke him to plague us with divers diseases and sundry kinds of death.' This is a far cry from the meal with Zacchaeus indeed! Such warnings rested on a misreading of a passage in Paul's first letter to Corinth (1 Corinthians 11.27–32) where he drew attention to the dire consequences of the failure of the members to respect one another as equals in Christ. Later generations unfortunately fetishized the bread and wine and thought the problem was not unjust relationships but 'unworthy receiving'. As we shall see in a moment, such a view runs counter to the deepest meaning of the eucharist.

Joy, gratitude and welcome characterize the description of the eucharist in the writings of the second-century apologists. The passing of another century finds a very different mood, and the character of the sign changes from a joyous meal which signifies God's making all things new to an

awesome sacrifice which atones for our sin. Perhaps by analogy with the rites of the mystery religions, great emphasis
was laid on the 'holy mysteries' which only initiates might
take part in. This theology received architectural expression
in the erection of the iconostasis or rood screen, which sep-
arated 'the sanctuary' from 'the people'. Whereas using the
eucharist has been the normal form of Christian worship for
the assembly on Sunday, the celebration of 'the holy mysteries' becomes less and less frequent. John Chrysostom, an
outspoken bishop of Constantinople in the fourth century,
speaks about 'the terrible sacrifice', the 'shuddering hour'
and 'the terrible and awful table' of the eucharist. One of
the chapters of his contemporary Basil the Great's *Shorter
Rule* is captioned: 'With what fear ... we ought to receive
the Body and Blood of Christ.' This feeling of awe led to a
rapid decline in the frequency with which people 'took
communion', the very idea of which marks a shift away
from the community which gathered for the Lord's
Supper to a spiritualized and privatized 'communing with
the Lord'. This led a church council in the sixth century to
insist on communion four times a year. The Fourth Lateran
Council of 1215 ratified a long-standing practice when it
made communion once a year sufficient.

Where the grace of Jesus' encounter with Zacchaeus was
a forgiving and welcoming fellowship, by this time emphasis fell increasingly on the 'miracle' of 'the change' –
transubstantiation – and grace was thought to be channelled
through that. If my argument is correct, however, a move
was made here which was fundamentally untrue to Jesus'
practice. The Reformers saw something of this, and
sought to get away from an 'altar' to 'the Lord's table', to
reverse the signification back to primitive practice. In one
way or another, however, it proved exceptionally difficult
to make this move. Anglicanism restored altar rails within

one or two generations. Presbyterianism surrounded the sacrament with as much awe as even the fourth-century Fathers could have wished. The motive was exemplary: to maintain the sense of holiness and reverence in worship. What we have to query is first, the understanding of holiness and second, how it is best expressed or signified. Grace is forgiving, accepting love. This was manifest in Jesus' table fellowship. It becomes a reality in the changed lives of outcasts who find themselves accepted and enabled to make a new start. Any parish priest knows of people who have excluded themselves from the eucharist for years because of feelings of 'unworthiness'. Quite apart from homilies like those in the Book of Common Prayer, this attitude was inculcated by the architecture and symbolism of the sanctuary.

'The beauty of holiness', however, is not that of the distant and mysterious God who 'comes down' to us in ritual practice but the beauty of forgiving love of which the eucharist ought to be the sacramental sign. In Catholic churches this was symbolized by the relation of the confessionals to the altar, but these dark boxes with their grilles precisely signified an intense privatization of religion. We know that in the Early Church 'confession' was an open avowal of failure and weakness, 'absolved' by the help and acceptance of the body of faithful people. In some quarters tentative steps have been taken to restore this practice which runs so deeply counter to the prevalent individualism of our culture and almost all churches have made far-reaching changes in their liturgies. Here at last the re-signification intended by the Reformers has been realized, and with the priest facing the congregation the meal aspect is once more emphasized over the sacrifice.

The habits of sixteen hundred years die hard, however, and we are perhaps still not clear enough that the eucharistic table is not for the worthy, as the Book of Common Prayer thought, but for the unworthy. When we line up to 'receive communion' we take our place behind Zacchaeus and the 'tax-collectors and sinners'. They are first in the queue, and we are not different from them. A beautiful Scottish story tells of a professor of Old Testament, and an elder of the kirk, who saw a girl bowing her head, unwilling to receive the sacrament. He pushed it into her hands saying, 'Tak it, lassie, tak it! It's fer sinners only!'

In my view it follows from this that we have to consider a possible reversal in the ancient church practice of insisting on baptism before receiving communion. This seemed to be called for by the structure of the gospel narrative, where the baptism comes at the beginning and the Last Supper at the end. We know that by at least the middle of the second century it was normal to proceed to the eucharist from baptism, and there is a certain logic in this. Baptism, according to Paul, is a sign of our dying and rising with Christ. It is a once-for-all step, a moment of commitment, our response to conversion, and also a mark that we have sought membership of the Church and been accepted. For this reason medieval churches have their fonts near the door of the nave, whilst a long, usually stepped, aisle leads up to the altar. However, if we allow the table fellowship of Jesus its proper place as part of the origin of our eucharistic practice we can see that baptism might well follow being received at table.

I was led to this view of the relation of baptism and eucharist by involvement in jail ministry in India. Across the road from the seminary where I worked in Madurai was a jail with more than a thousand prisoners. Week by week, students and staff from the seminary went over in the heat of a Sunday afternoon, sang hymns, preached, and celebrated the eucharist. About seventy prisoners attended, the vast majority Hindus. No bar was put on who could or who could not receive communion. Receiving communion, being accepted, was a sign of the gospel of forgiveness which had been preached. This activity was not part of any effort to 'convert' Hindus but nevertheless from it came a steady trickle of baptisms. What had happened was that Jesus' encounter with Zacchaeus had been relived: first table fellowship, then repentance and membership of the new community. This seems to me a far more beautiful and gracious practice than setting preconditions on coming to 'the Lord's table' – something the Lord never did.

If this is right then I believe it also bears on the vexed question of intercommunion. Many churches have a rule which allows communion to 'full members of any other church'. Others, however, and in particular the Roman Catholic Church, do not allow this. The original grounds for this refusal, as spelled out by the First Vatican Council more than a century ago, were that the Orders of other churches were 'invalid', and that the Roman Church was the only true Church, all others being in heresy and schism. Amongst members of that Church who are genuinely ecumenically inclined the reasons now given for continuing to refuse communion are that it is important not to fudge real doctrinal differences, and that it is necessary to 'bear the pain' of division until organic unity can once again be achieved. 'Truth' is sought in the most ungracious way possible – by refusing fellowship.

One respects the argument that both doctrine and the issue of truth are important. Liberation theologians have insistently asked what it means that the oppressor and the oppressed should come to the same table. Is this not papering over differences, sanctifying racism, class oppression and other inhuman ideologies in the name of religious unity? As one of them puts it, it seems to say that issues of suffering, violence, injustice, famine, and death are less critical and decisive than religious formulas and rites.[1] The question is how one deals with this problem (which is not just encountered in South America!) and the related issue of doctrinal difference. Do we proceed by exclusion – excommunication – a procedure the Church adopted very early on? If the eucharist stems from the table fellowship of Jesus, the redeeming of Zacchaeus and of goodness only knows how many ne'er-do-wells with connections with the local police chief, it seems unlikely.

This is not to say we bury differences in a sentimental, profoundly untruthful religious cosiness. It means that love of those with whom we differ, and who may even be our enemies, goes on *through* the table fellowship, not apart from it. How can we address sin by repeating it, by underscoring division, by introducing it into the table fellowship of Christ? To follow Christ, to be disciples, is to learn to deal with very *real* differences in the context of shared and forgiving table fellowship. I speak here especially of denominational differences. Those of us who live comfortable middle-class lives cannot speak for those for whom torture and death is a daily reality. Even there, I suspect, the question of apostasy or idolatry (which is what it comes down to, the claim that we are worshipping different gods) cannot be dealt with by exclusion.

To recall practices of exclusion is to be led to the current maelstrom of changing forms of relationship only too often met with, in the past, by exclusionary practices. The eucharist has both 'body' and relationship at its heart. How does it bear on these issues? When the Church of England produced its report on sexuality in 1995 the tabloid press led with the headline: 'Living in sin no longer sinful!' Many Christians feel that, above all in the area of sexual morality, the Church has simply trimmed with the wind. In his insistence that contraception cannot be used, and that abortion is impermissible except *in extremis* Pope John Paul II, some feel, has preserved Christianity's role as a counter-culture more faithfully.

There is no doubt both that we are living through an unparalleled renegotiation of the sexual contract between men and women, and a profound reorientation in our understanding of sexuality in general which affects our understanding of all human relationships. How does our eucharistic practice bear on all this? What are we to learn from the holiness of Jesus' praxis, which seemed so odd and unholy to many of his contemporaries ('a glutton and a drunkard!')?

Christians have always sought to derive the 'counsels of perfection' from their reflection on Jesus' life and death. Deep in the tradition is the notion that we can only attain holiness – and this is something to which all human beings, not just Christians, are called – by a war against the 'flesh' and the body. Paul wrote:

> Athletes exercise self-control in all things . . . So I do not run aimlessly, nor do I box as though beating the air; but I punish my body and enslave it, so that after proclaiming to others I myself should not be disqualified (1 Corinthians 9.25, 27).

What we have to ask ourselves is whether this idea of punishing and enslaving the body, which was taken to be the way in which we are to be 'crucified' to self, is the way to the holiness we see in Jesus' encounter with sinners. What emerges from that picture is that holiness is love irradiated by integrity. The radiance is not metaphorical but real, which is why medieval artists, more clear-sighted than we

27

are perhaps, painted haloes on saints and their figures of Christ. That integrity led Jesus to his death, but he did not go to death because he sought the punishment and enslaving of his body. There are some big negatives in Jesus' life: no to Mammon, no to relations of hierarchy and domination, for instance.

There is much more of affirmation, including, if we are to trust the hostile jibes which are recorded about table fellowship, affirmation of the body. This affirmation of the body, the other, and the self, as the way to holiness, is what is being explored in the new ways of relating. True, it seems a far cry from the bloody act of self-giving on the cross to the self-giving in erotic love, but as many of the martyrs and writers of Latin America have reminded us in the past forty years, these two frequently go together. Loving in integrity embraces the political, the erotic, and the depths of friendship, and we should not prise these modes of loving apart. If the eucharist stems, in part, from the table fellowship of Jesus, which is to say from part of his education of his disciples into the meaning of love, then I believe it has something to say to this maelstrom of renegotiated relationships in which we find ourselves. It is given us as sustenance and schooling in our apprenticeship in loving.

Our understanding of what might be entailed in such loving differs in some important respects from that of those who were disciples before us. For most Christian generations, for example, it has seemed that same-sex erotic relationships could not be blessed by God. For increasing numbers of contemporary Christians, on the other hand, there is the discovery that integrity and holiness can very decidedly be part of such relationships. All have followed their apprenticeship in the one 'body' of the eucharistic fellowship, nourished by the broken body given for us. What should not be an issue is the wholeheartedness, let us say the passion, with which both they and we have sought and seek to follow our apprenticeship. It is not that earlier generations knew about discipline whilst we do not. What has changed, as it changed for Bonhoeffer in his prison cell, is our understanding of discipline.

It is unfortunately true of apprentices that they bodge things and make countless mistakes, a fact we know theologically as 'sin'. No one knew this better than Jesus himself, and he addressed the fact sternly enough, but without identifying sin primarily with sexuality. On the contrary, 'sin' in his discourse is that whole network of practices which hinder our humanity by preventing us loving our neighbour. Certainly we can sin with and against our bodies and the bodies of others, and because we are disciples of the Word which takes flesh we are right to take such sin utterly seriously, but we have to ask what it is we do in the flesh which eclipses our humanness, which fails to respect the image of God in ourselves and our neighbour.

Could this be physical relations (what our society calls simply 'sex') between people of the same gender? It seems implausible, especially when we recognize that much Church teaching on sexuality springs from Aristotle's view of nature. He believed that every act and object had its own proper *telos* (end or purpose). When his philosophy was embraced by Aquinas it seemed clear that using things outside their proper *telos* was sin. The *telos* of sexual relations was procreation, so any form of sexual expression beyond that was sin. What has happened this century, after the invention of safe forms of contraception, is that our whole understanding of the *telos* of sexual relations has changed. For the whole of human history up to this century, sexual relations between men and women were bound up with conception, birth, the possibility of death in childbirth, high infant mortality rates, and so forth. We now understand sexuality much more in terms of mutual exploration, affirmation and celebration, and this applies equally to same-sex relationships. It is also true, of course, that the Church always recognized that the key barriers to integral loving which Jesus sought to throw down were 'pride' or self-righteousness, rather than sins of the flesh.

Jesus leaves us no rule book to guide us in discovering the reality of love for our neighbour. Those who construe Scripture in this way fall into the same trap as some of those with whom Jesus found himself locked in most perplexed and difficult debate, whom he had to warn about the 'sin against the Holy Spirit'. It is when we are certain we have the right answers that we are most unteachable. What we are shown in the gospel story is that love involves *concrete* practice, that it demands humility of spirit, and that it is quite incompatible with an attitude of wealth and security which throws a few crumbs to the poor. Apart from that we are left to an open, rigorous exploration of the patience and creativity of God's love in our own apprenticeship in loving. One of the set contexts for this happening is the eucharist.

The eucharist has been at the centre of Christian practice from the beginning because, in so many ways, it captures the heart of the Christian project. Paul summarized his understanding of that project in his contrast between two human situations, and in doing so was trying to spell out the significance of Jesus' word to his disciples that 'It shall not be so among you' (Mark 10.43 RSV). The situation of being 'in Adam', which did not end in AD 35 or thereabouts, but describes an ongoing human situation, is that of relationships of domination, hierarchy, division and the attempt to solve problems through law or violence. The situation of being 'in Christ' is that situation where there is 'no Jew or Greek, slave or free, male or female' – where, in other words, our status as friends under God is recognized. There is the old society, still very much with us, and very much part of the Church, in which power is exercised as 'the lords of the Gentiles' exercise it. The divisions and practices of exclusion which have defaced eucharistic practice, as so much of what the Church has done, only too painfully represent the old Adamic order. We need to find ways of representing and setting in our midst as a community a sign of our being 'in Christ', in the new order.

The problem is not new, for Paul already faced it in Corinth. The problem in Corinth was that the congregation was at loggerheads both between rich and poor and between men and women. From what we can gather, the congregation met in the house of one of the wealthier members, Erastus or Stephanas. Erastus may well be the person described by an inscription archaeologists have discovered as wealthy enough to pave one of the main streets in Corinth. Such rich people sauntered up from their offices and had some wine before the Christian gathering. 'Chloe's people', on the other hand, did not finish work till late and rushed up to the eucharist smelling of fish and bringing only a piece of pitta bread to eat. So the complaints Paul heard were that 'one goes hungry and another becomes drunk'(1 Corinthians 11.21). 'Do you show contempt for the church of God', asked Paul, 'and humiliate those who have nothing?' (11.22). To behave like this, said Paul, was to invite judgement on oneself, because it represented a fundamental disregard for the body. But have we not, for centuries, been guilty of precisely such disregard?

If this is the case, as I believe it is, it stems in part from the fact that we have narrowed the base for our understanding of the eucharist unduly. From a joyful and forgiving table fellowship we have turned it into either a mystery cult or something so solemn that sinners are not welcome there.

Surely it is clear that Jesus blew this trammelled religious world sky high! The Word he made flesh was that of God's love for sinners. It is this fresh, vibrant and creative word we have to rediscover in our eucharistic practice as a sign of hope for a world still racked by division.

3

The Great Economy

IN THE PREVIOUS chapter I have argued that our celebration of the eucharist does not derive only from the 'Last Supper' narrative but is also rooted in the table fellowship of Jesus, and that this has significant consequences for our understanding of our social world. In this chapter I shall argue that 'the great feedings', the feeding of the four thousand and the five thousand, are also an essential part of the practice of Jesus which gives us the eucharist, and that this bears directly on our existence as economic beings.

In the stories of the great feedings Jesus finds himself surrounded by a huge crowd late on in the day, and the problem arises how people are to be fed:

> When it grew late, his disciples came to him and said, 'This is a deserted place, and the hour is now very late; send them away so that they may go into the surrounding country and villages and buy something for themselves to eat.' But he answered them, 'You give them something to eat.' They said to him, 'Are we to go and buy two hundred denarii worth of bread, and give it to them to eat?' (Mark 6.35–7).

As Ched Myers has observed, Jesus challenges the disciples to use their imaginations, but they cannot.[1] They are bound by the framework of the market place. 'What are we supposed to do?' they ask. 'Go to the shops and buy huge quantities of bread and feed everyone?' The incredulity is exactly that of people today confronted by world poverty.

33

Jesus, however, has another proposal: 'Go and see how much bread there is.' In John's version it is a child who says that he has brought five rolls and a couple of fish (John 6.9). Jesus solemnly gives thanks to God, breaks and shares, as he did at all meals. What happens then? Traditionally theologians have believed in a miraculous multiplication of particles, through which the crowd was fed. It seems much more beautiful, and much more in keeping with the Jesus who refused signs to prove his messiahship, and resisted the temptation to turn stones into bread, to believe that the boy's artless willingness to share shamed others into sharing what they also had brought with them. When they do this it turns out that 'all ate and were filled' (Mark 6.42). 'The only "miracle" here is the triumph of the economics of sharing within a community of consumption over against the economics of autonomous consumption in the anonymous marketplace.'[2]

The eucharistic significance of the occasion was plain to the Early Church. Mark tells us that Jesus 'looked up to heaven', that he 'blessed', 'broke', and 'gave' – the actions of the eucharist, whilst John says that the crowd ate the bread, 'after the Lord had given thanks' (*eucharistesantos*).

In the history of the Church, the use and blessing of material elements in the eucharist has been taken as an affirmation of the material creation. Thus in the second century Irenaeus, Bishop of Lyons, speaks of the eucharist as thanksgiving for the blessings of creation. When we offer the bread and wine we remember that Christ is 'the Word through whom the trees bear fruit, the springs flow, and the earth yields "first the blade, then the ear, then the full corn in the ear"'.[3] This was a very important affirmation in Irenaeus' world, where Gnosticism, which despised the created order, came within a hairsbreadth of overwhelming orthodox Christianity. It is an even more important affirmation today in a world threatened as never before by piecemeal destruction through the misuse of the earth's resources and wholesale destruction through nuclear weapons. In its affirmation of the material the eucharist was and is a 'Green' sacrament, a sign of the God-given character of the material which is not there for human beings to pillage.

Green issues have attained prominence in the past thirty years partly through the campaigning efforts of groups like Greenpeace and Friends of the Earth and partly because of an increasing wealth of literature documenting the problem. To take one much publicized example, it has been predicted that global warming will cause ocean levels to rise with catastrophic results for many Southern hemisphere countries. The main cause of global warming is CO_2 emissions caused by Northern hemisphere consumption patterns. The average resident of an industrial country consumes three times as much fresh water, ten times as much energy, and nineteen times as much aluminium as someone in a developing country.[4] Dealing seriously with the problem has huge consequences for all those of us in the North. President Bush announced that 'The American way of life is not negotiable', but there is no choice but to deal with it, either by continued and increased violence against the South, or by changing our lifestyles. The earth cannot sustain present Northern consumption patterns for eight or eleven billion people.

In this context, Irenaeus' understanding of the eucharist, with its lyrical affirmation of the goodness of the earth, echoed in so many of our harvest hymns, takes on an entirely new urgency. The president of the eucharist takes and offers matter, and gives thanks for it. To do this seriously and worshipfully, which means responsibly, is to understand the eucharist as a commitment to a world where we appreciate God's gift, where it is not plundered or exploited, or cornered for the advantage of the few.

What Irenaeus did not mention was that the bread we offer is the fruit of human work, as the offertory sentence now affirms:

> Blessed are you, Lord of the Universe who gives us this bread, fruit of the earth and work of human hands. It will become for us the bread of life.

This reminds us that to produce the bread of the eucharist at least eight operations are necessary, from ploughing to marketing to baking. Each of these operations has a global economic, social and political dimension. Somebody pays somebody else to do the work. The work is done in competition or cooperation. In the global economy the production of grain is part of the balance of payments and the relation between nations. The bread of the eucharist is the bread of the economy. The liturgy is inescapably enmeshed in 'the real world' of the world economy. Let us see what is involved in that.

Innumerable recent reports and studies have drawn attention to the growing gap between the nations of the North and South, and to the growing gap between rich and poor within Northern hemisphere nations. I shall use one of the most recent of these, *The Oxfam Poverty Report*, which draws on a mass of field research from all over the world.[5] The report speaks of the 'silent emergency' of poverty which causes thirty-five thousand children to die *every day* from diseases which could be prevented through access to adequate nutrition and the most basic health provision. Poverty, the report concludes, is growing – not decreasing. All over the South, levels of real wages, health standards and expenditure on education are actually falling. Why is this?

A major cause of the poverty of the South is the asset-stripping which went on during the colonial era, but I will not go into that, but concentrate on contemporary factors. The Report of the World Commission on Environment and Development in 1987[6] maintained that 'Among the many causes of the African crisis, the workings of the international economy stand out.' Unfair trade, in one way or another, is at the heart of many of the problems.

To highlight just a few of the aspects this involves we can single out first the protectionism which persists despite the dogma of the so-called 'free market'. It has been said that the breakdown in the GATT system is nowhere more evident than in trade relations between developed and developing countries. 'Here an undeclared trade war is in progress.'[7] The European Community specifically discriminates against the three principal Third World exports – metals, agricultural products and textiles. The multi-fibre agreement, which aimed to protect the textile industries of the North against cheap imports from the South, has so far resisted all attempts to change it. The verdict of Belinda Coote, writing for Oxfam, is sombre:

> The GATT is often accused of being a club that regulates world trade to suit the interests of its most powerful members, particularly those of the USA and the EC ... The evidence to support these criticisms is overwhelming.[8]

Second, there is an obvious inequity between the commodity exports of the Third World and the manufactured goods of the First World. Demand for basic commodities grows only slowly and competition increases; they are sold on the market whereas tractors and turbines are sold on a cost-plus basis.[9] The introduction of artificial substitutes, sometimes prompted by a hike in Third World commodity prices – corn syrup for sugar, synthetics instead of cotton, plastics instead of timber – in turn affects the prices of raw materials. This means that each year there is a huge 'poor man's gift' to the rich through low commodity prices.

Third, there is the question of the role of transnational corporations, which now control between a quarter and a third of total world output and which account for 30 per cent of all world trade within themselves. It is often maintained that they benefit poorer countries by contributing to development, but, as the economists Singer and Ansari point out:

> A development process that is being sustained by organizations interested primarily in profit maximization is organically different from a development process in which the public sector sets the pace. The direct effect of the multinationals' investment is largely confined to the employment of a small, elite, semi-skilled and highly skilled labour force, the members of which earn incomes that are substantially higher than the incomes of the domestic labour class.[10]

Bhopal was a clear example of a case where the global reach of multinationals may be detrimental to the interests of the people of the South. So called 'Free Trade zones', of which there are now more than eighty operating in thirty countries, offer transnationals cheap non-union labour kept in check by harsh anti-strike legislation, a range of subsidies, and unrestricted repatriation of profits.

Investment by transnationals often diverts finance and energy away from the rural areas where most people live. Where it does not, however, as in the 'agribusiness' of the 'Green Revolution', the effects can be disastrous. The introduction of soya bean cultivation in Brazil, for example, has downgraded the quality of the local diet by occupying formerly food-producing land and causing prices to rise. The introduction of cash crops throughout sub-Saharan Africa has taken the most fertile land away from direct food production. 'In this way, they not only exploit the food crisis, but are significantly responsible for it in the first place'.[11] The high-technology export-crop model of agribusiness increases hunger because

> Scarce land, credit, water and technology are pre-empted for the export market. Most hungry people are not affected by the market at all … The profits flow to corporations that have no interest in feeding hungry people without money.[12]

Related to these problems is the question of debt, recently highlighted by Christian Aid. The present debt crisis of Third World countries began when OPEC countries deposited their new oil wealth in Western banks. Since idle money loses against inflation, the banks needed to find countries to take loans. At first, interest rates were low or even negative, but they leapt in the 1980s when the United States pushed up world interest rates as a response to trade and budget deficits. The World Commission report already mentioned notes that 'major changes in international conditions' made debts contracted in the early 1970s unsustainable and real wages have fallen and unemployment risen, with growing poverty and deteriorating environmental conditions throughout the South. The effects of Southern debt have been described as 'financial low intensity conflict'. A Brazilian Labour leader speaking in 1985 described this in these terms:

Without being radical or overly bold, I will tell you that
the Third World War has already started – a silent war,
not for that reason any the less sinister. This war is tearing
down Brazil, Latin America and practically all the Third
World. Instead of soldiers dying there are children, instead of millions of wounded there are millions of
unemployed; instead of destruction of bridges there is
the tearing down of factories, schools, hospitals and
entire economies ... a war by the United States against
the Latin American continent and the Third World. It is
a war over the foreign debt, one which has as its main
weapon interest, a weapon more deadly than the atom
bomb.[13]

The structural adjustment programmes imposed by the
World Bank are designed to generate wealth which will
then trickle down from rich to poor. However, far from
wealth trickling down to the poorest the living standards
of the rich and poor are diverging more and more widely.
Where, in 1960, the richest fifth of the world's population
had incomes thirty times greater than the poorest fifth they
now receive sixty times more. 'If poverty were an infectious
disease,' *The Oxfam Poverty Report* comments,

> which could be caught by the rich as well as the poor, it
> would have been eradicated long ago. Political will and
> financial resources would have been found in abundance,
> just as they were to develop instruments of mass destruc-
> tion during the Cold War. Yet governments, north and
> south, have been willing to tolerate and acquiesce in the
> steady marginalisation of the poor.[14]

Christianity is about alternatives: 'It shall not be so amongst
you.' When the president of the eucharist takes the bread

and breaks it, she offers an image of God's creation given to be shared equally amongst all of God's people. 'Blessed are you, Lord of the Universe', we say, referring to the whole of creation. The Kentucky farmer philosopher Wendell Berry speaks of the whole world system as 'The Great Economy', a whole within which there is ceaseless exchange. He points out that the world economy of GATT, the G7 summit and the world stock markets are only a tiny part of that. Its hubris is that it believes itself to be the whole and it exists by pillage of the great economy.[15]

Taking up this image, Ched Myers draws our attention to those sayings in Mark which focus on the impossibility of the rich entering the kingdom (10.23–5). Why? Because the kingdom is that situation where there *are no rich and poor*. The rich, therefore, whilst they are still rich, cannot enter, by definition. The rich man who comes to Jesus is told to redistribute all his wealth. Myers goes on:

Redistributive justice is high heresy in capitalism. But in the narrative of biblical radicalism, economic justice is the fundamental social goal of the people of God. The ancient vision of the Jubilee year ... was periodically to deconstruct debt, land alienation, and bond servitude – the three stages of impoverishment resulting from indebtedness ... We who have been socialized within the womb of capitalism dismiss such notions as utopian. True and universal economic justice, if it is contemplated at all, is done so as an eschatological hope; a noble ideal, but impossible to realize. But this attitude is precisely what is at issue in the conclusion to [the story of the rich man]. What is altogether impossible within our historical constructions is altogether possible within the reconstructive purview of God. Mark now argues that the hundredfold harvest promised in Jesus' sower parable

41

was not a pipe dream of indebted peasants but the concrete result of redistributive practice by the disciples
(10.28). Surplus is created when the entitlements of
household (basic productive economic unit), family
(patrimonial inheritance) and land (basic unit of wealth)
are 'left', i.e. restructured as community assets.[16]

Such a restructuring will involve, as this story in Mark in-
dicates, and as Jesus repeatedly emphasized, the disbelief of
the worldly wise and what he called 'moving mountains'.
In our world it involves no less than taking on the capitalist
system, as the philosopher Kai Nielsen, a sturdy opponent
of theism, has pointed out. Capitalism, he argues, requires,
and indeed can accept, at most a somewhat improved and
more efficient version of the present and that, in turn, requires great injustice and inhumanity. He goes on: 'If we
are morally serious and not ideologically blinkered, we
will realize that it is our central social task to get rid of capitalism.'[17] In this, surely, we have to agree with him. At the
beginning of the sixteenth century Bartolomeo de las Casas
already saw the connection between a situation of exploited
labour and the eucharist. A former slave owner, he was or-
dained and prepared to celebrate the eucharist. He found
this passage set for the reading:

> If one sacrifices ill-gotten goods, the offering is
>   blemished;
>   the gifts of the lawless are not acceptable.
> The Most High is not pleased with the offerings of the
>   ungodly,
>   nor for a multitude of sacrifices does he forgive sins.
> Like one who kills a son before his father's eyes
>   is the person who offers a sacrifice from the property
>   of the poor.

The bread of the needy is the life of the poor;
  whoever deprives them of it is a murderer.
To take away a neighbour's living is to commit murder;
  to deprive an employee of wages is to shed blood.

(Sirach 34. 21–7)

Hearing this stopped las Casas in his tracks. He abandoned
the eucharist to return to Spain to get a charter for the
Indians. He realised that the bread of the eucharist signifies
not just the good earth but also the human product, the fruit
of exploited labour. Bread which is taken from the poor
cannot be the bread of life, but is the bread of death. If we
in the North are offering the fruit of the life of the poor at
our eucharist we become like one who 'kills a son before his
father's eyes'. Such an offering cannot be acceptable to the
God and Father of Jesus Christ. It is only acceptable to the
Moloch who loves to feast on human blood, and who demands human sacrifice. In that case our worship is not
eucharist but idolatry, worship of Mammon.

The problem is that, since we are willy-nilly caught up in
structures of injustice, how is it possible to celebrate the eucharist? Should we be like the Colombian priest Camillo
Torres who refused to celebrate the eucharist until justice
had been achieved? Many may feel like that. Las Casas
offers another alternative. He committed his life to a struggle for the Indians. Is that not what sharing the eucharistic
bread calls us to? We take bread and wine, the product of
labour. We remember that these products represent the
'life' of those who made them, their time and creativity.
We remember especially that, in the words of Ben Sirach,
they are 'the life of the poor'. We remember that the
Church is a worldwide body, with people 'from every
nation', and that this 'one body' is split between haves and
have nots, just as it was at Corinth. We remember what

Paul said to that situation: that it involves us 'putting to shame those who have nothing'. In this remembering we celebrate with integrity, drawing our inspiration to work for change from our feeding on the bread of life.

But is a different economic world really possible or, as we are repeatedly told by 'realists' – is there no alternative? The answer to this is that there is of course an alternative where there is the political will to realize it. This would involve, in the first place, a whole series of democratic regulatory bodies, as proposed by the 1992 UN Development Programme.[18] The present World Bank could be replaced by a global central bank with the task of creating a common currency, maintaining price and exchange-rate stability, providing for a global adjustment of surpluses and deficits and for equal access to international loans. This was already suggested by Keynes in 1944 but rejected by the US. GATT could be replaced by an international trade organization to ensure free and equal access to all forms of global trade and manage commodity stabilization schemes. Instead of the present system of loans, development could be financed by a system of progressive income tax to be collected automatically from the rich nations and to be distributed to the poor nations according to their income and development needs. Finally we need the establishment of a new Development Security Council which could establish a broad policy framework for all global development issues, from food security to ecological security, and an International Court of Economic Justice responsible for the management of those resources on which we all depend. Urgent areas would be fish, water, and forests.

Not only are these policies, not pipe dreams – they are actually urgent and practical recommendations for the survival of the planet. If these considerations are not at the heart of our eucharist then we do indeed celebrate in vain. 'I hate,

I despise your festivals' said YHWH to the rich who lived in the lap of luxury whilst the poor starved (Amos 5.21). Those of us who live in the equivalent of houses of cedar must be careful we do not incur the same condemnation. Properly celebrated, the eucharist is a challenge to construct what the World Council of Churches has spoken of as a just, participatory and sustainable world order in which the poor are no longer fed with crumbs from the rich man's table. It is oriented essentially towards this future as it celebrates not only the God who is the source of our hope, but the God who in Godself hopes and hopes in us.

4

The Peaceable Kingdom

> Pray, brethren, that my sacrifice and yours
> may be acceptable to God, the almighty Father.

THIS IS THE introduction to the central prayer of the eucharist, the 'canon', in the Roman Catholic Church. By way of
explanation, the editors of *The Weekday Missal* write in their
introduction:

> At the Last Supper, Christ instituted the paschal sacrifice
> and meal. In this meal the sacrifice of the cross is continu-
> ally made present in the Church when the priest,
> representing Christ, carries out what the Lord did and
> handed this to his disciples to do in his memory.[1]

At the Reformation, the idea of the 'sacrifice of the mass'
was repudiated because it seemed to call in question the
'once for allness' of what was done on Calvary. On the
other hand, Christ's 'one, perfect and sufficient sacrifice,
oblation and satisfaction' remained the very heart of the
eucharistic prayer.

In the previous two chapters I have argued that our eucharistic practice stems not just from the Last Supper but
from Jesus' table fellowship and the great feedings as well.
Indisputably, however, the Last Supper narrative has been
the central text for understanding the eucharist from the
very beginning. How are we to understand it? The
Roman missal offers one widely accepted reading, differing
from Protestantism in the role it attributes to the priest, and

the way it understands *anamnesis* (recalling or memorial) but sharing the view that Christ's sacrificial death is the heart of the eucharist. It is clear that we cannot get away from the language of sacrifice, but the question is how we understand it. For this chapter I have borrowed a title from the Texan ethicist Stanley Hauerwas. Christ's death, I shall argue, is intended to introduce an order which is not based on violence – a truly alternative order. Many notions of sacrifice, on the other hand, retain ideas of violence within them.

'We have no shrines and altars.' This is from the apologist Minucius Felix, writing towards the end of the second century, and it is a common Christian watchword of the period. The eucharist is often spoken of as fulfilling Malachi's prophecy of a 'pure offering' (Malachi 1.11). 'Prayers and sacrifices performed by worthy men are the only perfect sacrifices pleasing to God', writes Justin.[2] It is the boast of the second-century Church that Christians differ from their pagan neighbours by *not* having propitiatory sacrifice, an offering, frequently an animal, designed to obtain God's favour and appease God's wrath. The eucharist, for these writers, is not itself a sacrifice though, as Rowan Williams has put it in an eloquent exposition of their views on sacrifice: 'The effect of Christ's sacrifice is precisely to make us "liturgical" beings, capable of offering ourselves, our praises and our symbolic gifts to a God who we know will receive us in Christ.'[3]

We first discern a change in the next century when Cyprian, in North Africa, writes:

If in the sacrifice which Christ offered none is to be followed but Christ, assuredly it behoves us to obey and do that which Christ did. For if Jesus Christ, our Lord and God, is himself the chief priest of God the Father, and has first offered himself a sacrifice to the Father and has

47

commanded this to be done in commemoration of himself, certainly that priest truly discharges the office of Christ who imitates that which Christ did; and he then offers a true and full sacrifice in the Church to God the Father, when he proceeds to offer it according to what he sees Christ himself to have offered.[4]

It seems that the emphasis has moved from the idea of moral sacrifice, and the sacrifice of praise and thanksgiving, to the idea that the bread and wine are themselves the sacrifice. The reasons for this change are quite unclear, but it led to profound changes in the celebration of the eucharist. Instead of the table from which both eucharist and common meal might be eaten is an altar. An altar requires a sacred place, and so it facilitates the change from an ordinary house to a sacred building. In understanding the sacrifice, Cyprian appeals to Old Testament models. Increasingly Levitical models of priesthood are now adopted. The president of the assembly is replaced by a priest who must offer sacrifice, and who is dressed in special priestly garments to do so.

Two further changes are noteworthy. In the fourth century, the eucharist is increasingly described in terms similar to those used by the mystery religions. We have already seen how the early emphasis on the joy of fellowship with the Risen Lord is replaced by a new emphasis on awe and fear.

The second change relates to the new situation of the Church which began with the conversion of Constantine in 315 and was endorsed when Christianity became the official religion of the state under Theodosius at the end of the fourth century. The last great persecution occurred under Diocletian in 303/4, and right up to that time the Church was in no position to put up great buildings and conduct ostentatious liturgies. Many pagans referred with scorn to the low status of those who became Christians. At least one ex-slave became pope in Rome, and the worship of the first three centuries was generally that of a poor community which might at any time have to 'go underground' in the face of persecution. Once the emperor had become Christian, however, there were new demands. It was obviously inappropriate to worship God in a poor building when the emperor lived in a palace. It was inappropriate to celebrate with humble vessels when the emperor supped off gold and silver. And so began the tradition of great buildings and liturgical magnificence, the clothing of the priest in gorgeous brocades to honour God the sovereign of all, and the production of exquisite chalices and patens of precious metals studded with jewels. How strange and novel this idea was can be seen from the behaviour of Ambrose who, although he had a high doctrine of the 'real presence' unhesitatingly had the Church vessels melted down to ease the lot of the poor during the Gothic invasion, explaining that the poor were the real treasure of the Church.

These changes in the third and fourth centuries were decisive for what followed for more than one thousand years. The doctrine of the 'real presence', already firmly entrenched in the Church, found cogent elucidation in terms of an analogy from Aristotle's metaphysic of substance and accident. Just as, when we look at a chair, what we see is, say, brown, hard and shiny, but the underlying substance is not visible, so it could be said of the eucharistic elements that their 'accidents' – what we see, touch and taste – remained the same, but their substance became the body and blood of Christ. The 'change' was bound up with the idea of the re-presentation of Christ's sacrifice for sin on Calvary. Transubstantiation and eucharistic sacrifice went together.

That the bread and wine were truly Christ's body and blood meant that tremendous care had to be taken to see that crumbs of bread were not dropped, nor drops of wine spilt. This concern led eventually to the denial of the cup to lay people. As partaking at the eucharist was now infrequent, adoration of the consecrated wafer, the 'host' (from Latin *hostias* meaning sacrifice) replaced it. Lay people gathered, often outside the church door, or looked through 'squint holes' in the rood screen, to watch the miracle far away at the high altar, the mystery emphasized through vestments, bells, incense and a clerical language. The priest stood with his back to the people and as the host was lifted high above his head the people genuflected and adored the mystery of God's presence in the sacrament, imaging the broken body and shed blood on the cross. Priests were required to celebrate daily but the corporate dimension of the eucharist was lost. The eucharist became the supreme form of intercessory prayer, a repetition of the great sacrifice for sin.

These developments did not go without protest during the Middle Ages. At the Reformation a certain restoration of primitive practice was effected. In some communions the altar again became a table. Cranmer wanted it in the centre of the congregation, which was the point of what later became 'north end' celebration. Communion in both bread and wine was restored to the laity and the liturgy was celebrated in the vernacular. But the late medieval emphasis on the death of Christ was not overcome. For Protestantism in general the Holy Communion was a memorial of Christ's death for sin. Much of the music written to accompany the Protestant communion was set in a minor key, calculated to call up sad and meditative thoughts. Both Luther and Calvin wanted the eucharist as the normal form of Christian worship on Sundays, but suspicion of 'the mass' as a piece of popery made this difficult. Calvin was overruled by the city council in Geneva, which allowed it once a month. In many Protestant communions it was fixed at four times a year and church members were required to 'receive communion' only three times. The freedom of the early thanksgiving prayers was not recaptured.

The language of sacrifice is not dispensable – it touches roots too deep in human beings. The question is how we are going to understand it. We have seen that, in the second century, it applied above all to the sacrifice of praise and thanksgiving. To take this further we need to turn once again to the Last Supper narrative, remembering that we must not read it in isolation from the rest of the gospel story. The fact that Jesus' last act with his disciples was to share a meal is hardly a surprise, given the importance he attached to the sharing of food. In addition, this meal may well have had special significance, not just because Jesus could see his imminent arrest in view, and the likely outcome of that, but because, according to the Synoptics, it was a Passover meal. John depicts it as happening on the night before Passover but he has a theological motive for this, as he can then align the death of Jesus with the slaying of the Passover lamb. The case for the Passover dating, however, though strong, is not conclusive, and we have to be content with the fact that paschal ideas were bound to have been in the disciples' minds.

Of the four accounts of the meal, those of Luke and Paul seem to stand together on the one hand, and those of Matthew and Mark on the other. Mark is usually considered the oldest text on account of its semitisms and the difficulty of some of its expressions.[5] All four agree that Jesus 'blessed' bread before sharing it, and Luke and Paul's use of *eucharistein* rather than *eulogein* to describe this may well be intended to make clear to Gentiles what is meant by a Jewish blessing, which is thanksgiving. This thanksgiving, which accompanied every meal, was not a consecration prayer in the later sense but rather expressed a sense of the holiness and givenness of everyday life. According to Mark there followed a word of interpretation over the bread – 'Take, this is my body' – and after the meal over the cup – 'This is my blood of the covenant, which is poured out for many' (Mark 14.22, 24). The Luke/Paul tradition adds, 'Do this in remembrance of me' or 'Do this that God may remember me.'

What do these commands mean? Do what in remembrance of me? We have already seen that Jesus does not seem to have been the man for rituals. In Jewish tradition 'blood' is the 'life' (Leviticus 17.11) and as body and blood here stand in parallelism it may well be that Jesus is referring to his life offering. When Jesus tells his disciples to 'do this', therefore, it may have the larger meaning: 'Let the breaking and sharing of your continued table fellowship remind you of how my life was broken and poured out for God's purposes of salvation, and may you do likewise.' The eucharist is therefore rooted in the whole practice of Jesus in the sense of what he did and the culmination of that doing on the cross. There is, therefore, a second sense of sacrifice, bound up with but going beyond praise and thanksgiving. Sacrifice here is self-offering for the sake of God's kingdom.

Augustine seems to have understood it in this way in the fifth century. 'It is your mystery which is placed on the table', he said in a sermon. 'You hear the words, "the body of Christ"; you answer "Amen". Be a member of Christ, so that the "Amen" may be true.'[6] As we have noted, in the Middle Ages, and continuing into the Reformation, attention was focused on Jesus' death as a sacrificial atonement for sin. But the emphasis in the narratives is less on death as such and more on a life lived to the uttermost for others, even to the limits of death. John and the author of Hebrews both stress this in their insistence on the obedience of Jesus, and this is consonant with the scene in Gethsemane which immediately follows, where Jesus prays, 'Remove this cup from me; yet, not what I want ...' (Mark 14.36). The stress is not on the death as such, but on a self-offering which may involve death. This is consistent with both the scene in Gethsemane, and the emphasis on Jesus' obedience in Hebrews. The Greek text has 'do this' (*touto*) and not 'do thus' (*houtos*) and it seems that in this solemn and crucial moment Jesus sums up and refers to the whole movement of his life given for the kingdom he proclaimed. It is following him in 'this' which has to be 'done' by those who would follow him.

All our earliest traditions preserve the memory that Jesus spoke of the 'new covenant' at the Last Supper. In a way characteristic of the rabbis, the allusion was complex. What was probably in mind was Jeremiah's new covenant (Jeremiah 31.31–4), a covenant written on the heart which needed no animal sacrifice. Jesus, however, also invokes the ancient imagery of animal sacrifice, which sealed the covenant in early Israel (see, for example, the story in Genesis 15). Both aspects were reinterpreted as Jesus speaks of the inauguration of the new relationship between God and God's people through his commitment to the bitter end, even to death. This is the probable meaning of the 'blood shed, or poured out, for many'. Given that Jesus followed a man who had been executed (John the Baptist), that he was confused with him, and also identified with the prophets to whom Jewish tradition at the time popularly ascribed martyrdom (Luke 13.34), it is most likely that Jesus expected his death. How did he understand this? What kind of significance did he attach to it? I have already suggested that the words about 'my body and blood' may be understood as referring to his whole life offering. Did he think that his death would atone for sin? It is true that the Jewish world of his time attributed atoning significance to most deaths, especially those of martyrs, so it is not in the least implausible that Jesus attributed such a significance to his own death. A particularly attractive suggestion interprets Jesus' death for 'many' not as signifying abstractly 'all humanity' but the Gentiles for whom, according to tradition, there was no atonement.[7] On this account Jesus goes to his death, therefore, to inaugurate the messianic mission to the Gentiles, to embrace the Gentiles within God's promises, to make them inheritors of the promises of the Fathers. In his life and death he initiates a movement which will culminate in the kingdom of God, when he will once more be able to celebrate not only with his disciples but with the great crowd they have brought with them, at the messianic banquet of the nations.

Though I grant that this is both attractive and plausible I wish to make an alternative suggestion, based on the understanding of sacrifice in the Hebrew Bible. The way we talk about 'the Bible', especially if we want to go on and say, 'the Bible is God's Word', disguises the extent to which there is debate and disagreement within Scripture. It seems to me there is a twofold tradition about sacrifice in the Hebrew Bible, and that Jesus opts for one of them over against the other.

The tradition which has fed in to conventional interpretations of the eucharist is represented above all by Leviticus. There, animal sacrifice is needed to atone for sin and guilt. Unless sin and guilt are atoned for God's anger will be visited on Israel. There is no doubt whatever that this understanding of sacrifice goes back a very long way, perhaps to the roots of human culture, but it is also very important to realize that these texts were edited during the exile. The exile, which marked the end of the Davidic kingdom, was the most traumatic event in Israel's history. God had promised that Jerusalem and the house of David were inviolate; now they were destroyed. Why? What had happened? The answer was found in Israel's disobedience. How was such a catastrophe to be avoided in the future? Obedience was the obvious answer, but perfect obedience seemed impossible. The redactors of Leviticus represent a theology which recast the old traditions of propitiation and of the scapegoat to say that God has given Israel this form of sacrifice as a means to wipe out guilt, to turn away its destructive consequences. It is a properly sacramental understanding. God ordains that lifeblood may function in this way, though it was perfectly well understood that this kind of sacrifice could not atone for any sin whatsoever. Its scope was limited; it did not atone for sins committed with a high hand; but so far as it went it was a gracious means for avoiding the kind of punishment the exile was seen to represent.

The earliest text we have which speaks of the other tradition about sacrifice is the terrible story of 1 Samuel 15. Commanded to wipe out the Amalekites, to commit genocide, Saul spares the flocks and herds and the king. The prophet Samuel greets him with the words: 'Behold, to obey is better than to sacrifice, and to heed than the fat of rams' (1 Samuel 15.22).

He then hews 'Agag in pieces before the Lord' and commands the destruction of the sheep. Despite the terrible context I believe it summarizes a whole reading of sacrifice which insists that true sacrifice consists in obedience to God's commands. When it is echoed later by prophets like Amos, Hosea and Micah, and by the Psalmists it is always insisted that what God wants are works of mercy and justice. Amos may stand for all. He represents God asking, 'Did you bring to me sacrifices and offerings the forty years in the wilderness, O house of Israel?' (5.25).

Will the Lord be pleased with thousands of rams,
    with ten thousands of rivers of oil? ...
He has told you, O mortal, what is good;
    and what does the Lord require of you
but to do justice, and to love kindness (*chesed*),
    and to walk humbly with your God? (Micah 6.7–8)

In a text which Jesus quotes twice (Matthew 9.13; 12.7) Hosea puts these words into God's mouth: 'I desire steadfast love (*chesed*) and not sacrifice' (Hosea 6.6).

Paul, too, understood the Christian movement to involve the affirmation of this tradition of sacrifice: 'Present your bodies as a living sacrifice', he says to the Christians in Rome after his long rehearsal of the grace of God which has met them in Christ (Romans 12.1). The 'spiritual worship' of Christians consists in lives lived in obedience in response to grace, God's self-giving. The letter to the Hebrews represents a systematic exposition of this tradition. The blood of animals was really useless, says the author, as it clearly did not touch our lives. What was needed was Jesus' offering of *obedience* (Hebrews 5.8). Reflecting on the two traditions he says: 'He abolishes the first in order to establish the second' (Hebrews 10.9). It is by Christ's *will* that we are sanctified, not by his sacrificial blood. Blood is only a metaphor for obedience.

As we have seen, second-century writers continue Jesus' and Paul's option for the second tradition. The sacrifice we offer, they say, is one of thanksgiving and obedience. Only in the third century is Christ's death read in terms of the Levitical tradition.

It is true, of course, that there are many sacrificial allusions, and much use of sacrificial metaphor, in the New Testament. An intense pamphlet war raged throughout the eighteenth century as to whether this meant we should understand Christ's death sacrificially or not. Like most pamphlet wars it generated more heat than light but at least it becomes clear that there is no *compulsion* to read these texts as endorsing vicarious sacrifice. They can all be understood, as I have argued above, in terms of Christ's self-offering to the uttermost.

One problem with reading them in terms of vicarious sacrifice has recently been highlighted by the French anthropologist René Girard. Mimesis – imitation or copying – is fundamental to human activity. Unfortunately it generates violence, since it means we all want the same things and cannot all have them. Sacrifice, in Girard's view, is a way of dealing with that violence. It does so by scapegoating, which is ultimately a form of collective violence. In the scapegoat ritual a person, and later on an animal, is chosen as the symbolic focus of all the community's rage and anger. In the rite set out in Leviticus 16 the whole community throws stones at the goat until they drive it to its death over a precipice. This act of collective aggression is a kind of bloodletting which is designed to keep the community free of violence until next time.

Jesus, in Girard's view, saw that violence was the key human problem. Girard makes sense of two verses which leave conventional New Testament scholarship stumped. In Matthew's Gospel Jesus says: 'I will open my mouth to speak in parables; I will proclaim what has been hidden from the foundation of the world' (Matthew 13.35). The last phrase is repeated in Luke's account of Jesus' dispute with the scribes:

> Therefore also the Wisdom of God said, 'I will send them prophets and apostles, some of whom they will kill and persecute', so that this generation may be charged with

the blood of all the prophets shed since the foundation of
the world. (Luke 11.49–50)

The secret Jesus will reveal, says Girard, is the secret of
human violence, enshrined and sanctified in the sacrificial
system. Christ's mission was to uncover the secret of the
scapegoat mechanism, and to establish a human community
based on peace rather than violence. This constitutes the
very heart of Christian revelation and it is what is truly redemptive in Christianity. Unfortunately, from the very
earliest days, from the writing of the letter to the Hebrews,
Christianity betrayed its master, re-instituting Christ as the
supreme sacrificial victim. To do this was once again to
legitimate the violence of the scapegoat mechanism.
According to Girard, 'Historical Christianity took on a per-
secutory character as a result of the sacrificial reading of the
Passion and Redemption.'[8]

Both as an explanation of human violence, and as an account of sacrifice, there is no doubt that Girard's thesis is
simplistic. Nevertheless, Girard has done a great service by
drawing attention to the immense violence implicit in the
traditional reading of the passion stories. As many feminist
theologians have also argued, understandings of Christ's
death as a 'perfect sacrifice' have functioned to underwrite
sadomasochistic views of the self, and violence within society. The God who suffers as the scapegoat has validated
scapegoating. This theology has encouraged the view that
there is something valuable or redemptive about suffering
per se, and this has been used to insist that the poor, and especially women, should bear with and put up with all sorts of
things they should not have put up with.

Further, no matter how sophisticated the understanding
of expiation it has also been difficult to get away from a picture of God who needs the death by torture of the Son in

order to forgive humankind. This grotesque view of God has rightly seemed morally repulsive to many.

Finally, it has also underwritten the idea that we have to 'pay' for our sins by suffering. The eighteenth-century 'penitentiary' drew heavily on this strand of 'Christian' thinking. Jesus' distinctive emphasis on the re-creative nature of forgiveness has thereby been lost.

Girard is surely right, by contrast, to insist that Jesus stood for an alternative which was peace and not violence, forgiveness rather than punishment, friendship rather than excommunication. The kingdom he preached was the fulfilment of Isaiah's vision of creation at peace, where the wolf will lie down with the lamb, the leopard with the kid, the calf with the lion, and a nursing child shall lead them – the peaceable kingdom (Isaiah 11.6–8). This is another part of Jesus' alternative which the Church has found too difficult to live with. Much easier to retreat to a sacrificial liturgy than to live sacrificially to establish peace in the world!

What we have to take from the rehearsal of Jesus' death, therefore, is to recognize that the kind of sacrifice Jesus endorsed, the offering of our lives for others, for the marginalized, the weak, the victims of violence, may be necessary to usher in that kingdom. This is not to make a virtue out of suffering. How could the One who came to bring fullness of life to all possibly do that? It is to recognize that in the contest for fullness of life, for the right to feast and drink, as Jesus loved to do, it may be necessary to take on the powers that be and to die. To be faithful to the economic reading of the eucharist we may need to 'imitate' Christ's 'sacrifice' – his life given for the kingdom.

It is in this context that we can understand the command to 'remember'. Jeremias argues that the phrase looks back to Old Testament usage, and to the Passover liturgy, and is not a request for the disciples to 'remember' (for how are they likely to forget?), but for them to petition God to 'remember' God's people and God's promises. Thus at the Passover the head of the family prayed for 'the remembrance of us, our fathers, the Messiah and your holy city Jerusalem'.[9] In the same way Jesus asks his disciples to pray that God will remember his Messiah and the movement to the kingdom he initiated. 'By coming together daily for table fellowship in the short period before the parousia, and by confessing Jesus as their Lord, the disciples re-present the initiated salvation work before God and pray for its consummation.' Perhaps not daily but weekly, which was the ancient, and is now the modern practice, our eucharist is prayer for the coming of the peaceable kingdom, and a step on the road to its realization.

5

Fashioning Community

SINCE THE TIME of Homer's *Odyssey*, at least, (probably *c.*1000 BC) absence from home, and the return home, has been a metaphor for the human condition. Odysseus, who is 'Everyman', journeying through all the difficulties and dangers life can throw at him, facing temptation and death, returns to Penelope, who is keeping the hearth for him. He is so changed that only his old nurse can recognize him. After the suitors are killed, and Penelope has at last recognized him, the two are left together, but he has to tell her that Tiresias forecast that he will soon have to leave again: 'I must pass through many cities, holding in my hands a balanced oar till I come to men who know nothing of the sea, who eat food unseasoned with salt and are unacquainted with ships and their crimson cheeks.'[1] Homer seems to be saying that 'home' is more of a longing and a goal than a stable condition.

In the Hebrew Scriptures, the narrative of the 'promised land' fulfils the same function. From Genesis to the last of the prophets, Israel's story turns on arrival, exile, dispossession, longing:

> How could we sing the Lord's song
>   in a foreign land?
> If I forget you, O Jerusalem,
>   let my right hand wither!
> Let my tongue cling to the roof of my mouth,
>   if I do not remember you,
> if I do not set Jerusalem
>   above my highest joy (Psalm 137.4–6).

61

Rootedness – the vision of every family 'under its vine and under its fig tree' is the human dream – but the experience of exile is the reality. For some, like the author of Ecclesiastes, it is exile which has become a metaphor for the whole human condition, and 'home' is the long sleep of death: 'all must go to their eternal home, and the mourners will go about the streets' (Ecclesiastes 11.9f.).

A different experience of exile is signalled by the industrial revolution. In Britain at the start of the eighteenth century, five million people lived for the most part in tiny rooted communities where families intermarried over generations and local knowledge was profound, as it is in all peasant communities. The growth of the great cities, still continuing apace in Asia and Latin America, marked the beginning of a social dislocation with which we are still living. In this context the domestic hearth was extolled as the most sacred site of the human drama, most famously in this piece of doggerel from 1823:

Mid pleasures and palaces though we may roam,
Be it ever so humble there's no place like home;
A charm from the skies seems to hallow us there
Which, seek through this world, is ne'er met with elsewhere.

The growing sense of alienation in Western society was vividly imaged in all forms of art: in the paintings of Eduard Munch from 1894 onwards, in 'the moment of cubism' in 1907, and in Schoenberg's abandonment of triadic harmony and tonality in 1908. These movements in music and painting, echoed later in T. S. Eliot's *The Wasteland*, vividly express the sense that north European human beings are no longer at home in their world. The much discussed sense of crisis in family life is but a reflection of this larger sense of alienation.

The loss of community is one of the key themes of contemporary complaint, and it generates a search for, or nostalgia for, community. People hark back to a supposedly more friendly and intimate earlier age, before technology and before the big city. Before we allow ourselves to be carried away on a tide of heritage industry sentiment, we need to ask ourselves whether there ever was any such community. In the first place, though rooted communities undoubtedly existed for many centuries it is not so clear that they formed a more humane environment than our own. If we think of the way old women could be persecuted as 'witches', and those who refused to conform could be marginalized or victimized, not to mention the class oppression implicit in gentry–peasant relations, we can see that there was a great deal wrong with that world too.

In the second place, we have to be cautious about the idea that rootedness is the norm for human beings. English communities were very stable from the eleventh century to the eighteenth, but prior to that there were centuries marked by successive waves of invasions, and a wider view of human history evidences plenty of mass migrations, not to mention the existence of nomadic cultures. In his famous study *Attachment and Loss* John Bowlby even surmised that the reason crying babies fall asleep when we walk with them is to do with our nomadic past.[2] Perhaps settled communities are more the exception than the rule, more the substance of dreams than of reality.

What seems to have replaced the settled community for those of us in the industrialized world is the community of the network, so that we all exist within webs or networks of relationships based on work, leisure, or political interest groups. For many people, 'church' is just another such group, and it has to be said that it probably is one of the organizations which works hardest to build community wherever it finds itself and as such it is profoundly life-enhancing. We have already seen, however, that community as such is not necessarily good. Whilst it is certainly 'not good that man should be alone', communities can also be deeply destructive when their common energy is turned against an enemy – Serb against Muslim, for example, or Protestant against Catholic. Exploring the community issue further, we come up against the political.

Aristotle suggested that the peculiar dignity of humans was that they could choose the kind of community they wished to live in, and this is what he meant by 'politics'. Of course, in his world neither women nor slaves had any part in this choice. For some time now 'choice' has been a key political watchword, theoretically available for every adult citizen, but we know that our choices are constricted and directed in all sorts of fundamental ways, by education, environment, poverty, the power of the media and of advertising to name but a few. That we are 'free to choose' means that, in the Western liberal democracies at least, we will not have the secret police call for us so long as we play the game. This is not true, of course, for thousands of people in Ecuador or Guatemala today, and in many other countries in South America and the Third World in general.[3] Our freedom to choose, then, is a complex and threatened freedom but nevertheless Aristotle is right. In the non-trivial sense, politics is about our common human struggle to fashion more life-giving forms of community. But this, too, is the concern of the eucharist.

The contrast between the spiritual and the material, the religious and the political, in our culture, might still leave some people nervous about the claim that the eucharist has a political dimension, even when politics is described in terms of the fashioning of community. It is often said that Jesus, and the New Testament, are 'non-political'. There is truth in this. Jesus was not a signed-up party member. He did not have a brief either for the Romans (like the Sadducees) or against them (like the Zealots). This is, however, very different from saying that, if politics is about the kind of community we want, he was indifferent to that question. On the contrary, his talk about the kingdom is precisely about a new type of community, run according to quite different principles from both those of the 'lords of the Gentiles' and those exclusivists who believed God's promises stopped with Israel.

There are other reasons, too, for saying that the eucharist is inescapably political. We have seen that the Last Supper was, if not a Passover meal, then celebrated in a Passover context. The Passover celebrated the liberation of Israel from Egypt and the 'words of consecration' represent Jesus' reflections on that story. It was at Passover that nationalist feeling reached fever pitch and at this season the Romans always expected, and often got, trouble. This helps to explain why Pilate acted as he did in crucifying Jesus. When Jesus was arrested, his co-religionists handed him over to the Romans for a political trial. The inscription on the cross announced the cause of his punishment: Jesus was crucified as a messianic pretender, as a king other than Caesar.

As John above all realizes, there is a profoundly ironic truth in this accusation. The gospel reader knows that Jesus has done everything he could to avoid being confused with the kind of messianic pretender who wanted to mount an armed revolt against the Romans. On the other hand, the history of the Church in the first three centuries made clear that the refusal of legitimacy to Roman imperialism was a profoundly subversive act, and played its part in the fall of the Roman empire. All the self-serving imperial myths about the *pax Romana* and Rome's divine calling were simply undermined. The irony of Pliny's examination of Christian slaves, then, is that they were much more dangerous than he realized. Even today confession of Christ's Lordship constitutes a permanent question to all political power systems, challenging their tendency to overstep the limits of their power, a truth which was the foundation of the German Confessing Church's Barmen Declaration in 1934.

The eucharist is also inescapably political because, in the framework of liberal democracies, every person who comes to the Lord's table does so as one who makes a political option. Many people like to say they are 'a-political' but in general what this means is that they are satisfied with the way things are. Usually people are interested in the kind of medical attention available to them, the kind of education available to their children, the kind of job opportunities there are, and whether they are able to live without threats of violence either from thugs, hooligans, the army, or the police. All these are political concerns. Every person who comes to the eucharist has therefore a political option, and the option not to make an option is itself an option.

Protestant Christians are especially prone to the idea that life can be compartmentalized. Luther taught that there were two kingdoms, that of God and that of this world, and they both had their own autonomy. This was important in relation to the medieval Church's attempt to control everything: it effected a very necessary de-sacralization of politics, obstructing the notion that our human political order is identical with God's. Later on, during the Enlightenment, came the idea that whilst politics was the affair of the community religion was the affair of the individual. This too represented an important insight, coming as it did after a century of religious persecutions, but it fostered a schizophrenic attitude to life, the idea that life was a series of watertight compartments and this is clearly both untrue and potentially damaging.

If we compartmentalize our lives, we run the risk of persuading ourselves that there might be things we can do in the political sphere which we would not do in the private. This was one of the issues under scrutiny at Nuremberg. We tend to think of ourselves as workers in one part, parents or children in another, hobbyists in another, and lovers in another, but we are not lots of different people but one worker–lover–parent.

So it is all of us that comes to the eucharistic table, not just the religious part. I do not have, among other identities, a political identity and a religious identity. God encounters me as the one person I am. I do not come to the eucharist to escape from sordid political reality and get in touch with some quite different spiritual reality, but to find the one reality which frames my whole life interpreted, refracted and made more hopeful. The eucharist itself teaches me that I can only come to Truth, ultimate reality, through material – political, social, economic – means. Of this the bread and wine are a sign.

In a sense this is signified by the description of the eucharist as 'the mass'. This name comes from the last words of the Latin service: *'Ite, missa est'*, 'Go, it is the dismissal'. It reflects the point that the eucharist is not introverted, a wallow in religious sentiment, but extroverted; that Christians only gather in order better to perform their task in 'the world'. The whole eucharist leads up to the dismissal – that is its point. 'What would be the meaning of fifty-two masses celebrated in a year', asks the Sri Lankan theologian Tissa Balasuriyea, 'if there was no improvement for the poor in their shanties?'[4] 'Mass' means the eucharist exists for a more human world, but such a world does not come by daydreaming. 'Wishers were ever fools', says Shakespeare's

Cleopatra. It comes only through the rough and tumble of politics, tiresome, boring and arduous though these be (Oscar Wilde remarked aptly that the trouble with socialism was that it cost too many evenings).

If politics, then, is about fashioning a more human community, how does the eucharist contribute to that? Our faith shapes us, I believe, by educating our desire. It is our political compass, if not our map. To say that the eucharist is inescapably political does not mean that it is a political meeting. It does mean that in the eucharist Word and sign are brought to bear on real issues, on issues that affect the life and quality of life of others and myself. I come to the gathering round the Lord's table as political–religious–familial, body–mind–spirit whole person, in search of a deeper wholeness, to hear a Word which vitally concerns the very marrow of the world in which I live, and necessarily, therefore, a word about fashioning community. In the eucharist we are not pointed to any old community but to one characterized by sharing, by the overcoming of boundaries, by friendship.

Our very word 'community' has roots in the key New Testament word *koinonia*, usually translated 'fellowship' or 'communion', which gives us one of the most familiar descriptions of the eucharist in English. 'Holy communion' – both the communion of the 'saints', as Paul called the very imperfect members of Corinth or Galatia or Philippi, and their sharing in 'holy things'. *Koinonia* is one of the central characteristics of the young community. In a passage which has had immense significance for radical social groups through the centuries we read: 'Now the whole group of those who believed were of one heart and soul, and no one claimed private ownership of any possessions, but everything they owned was held in common' (Acts 4.32).

From the start, fellowship with Christ (1 Corinthians

1.9), sharing (the same word) in the blood of Christ (1 Corinthians 10.16) works itself out practically in the sharing of
resources with other communities (2 Corinthians 8.4; 9.13).
It is a paradox which must give peculiar satisfaction to the
devil that a word which has its origin as a description of the
common life has become privatized in the idea of 'receiving'
or 'taking' communion, where 'communion' seems to refer
just to the elements. The gift of the Holy Spirit, according
to Paul, was not given for our private satisfaction, or to
enable us to experience the delights of religious ecstasy, but
is 'for the common good' (1 Corinthians 12.7). In the most
famous of his metaphors, which was actually a political
commonplace of the time, Paul speaks of the *ecclesia* as a
body, all the parts of which work together for the good of
the whole.

It is not only resources which must be shared, but
common wisdom. In this respect it really is about time we
asked whether the sermon is the best way for our day-to-
day (political) lives to be illuminated by the word of Scripture within the eucharist. The sermon goes back to a time
when most 'hearers' were illiterate and the priest very
likely the most educated member of the community. This
has long since ceased to be the case. Of course, there is a
place for the sermon on some occasions – at rites of passage,
or on great festivals. When they are the norm, however,
they represent a very unbiblical refusal of the richness and
variety of the gifts of wisdom available in the community.
We urgently need to find ways of sharing that wisdom
within our liturgy.

Earlier this century, the sociologist Ernst Troeltsch characterized the experience of the Early Church as 'love
patriarchalism'. As such, he thought that it offered people
an alternative within their religious groupings, but posed
no challenge to society as a whole. This, it seems to me,

misses the point of Paul's language about the *ecclesia* – which we must not too readily translate 'Church' because of all the historical baggage that term carries with it. A much better translation would be 'the new society'. The Church was not intended, in Paul's thought, to constitute a little group of saved in the midst of a wicked world. On the contrary, as the universal dimension of his Adam–Christ language shows, Paul had nothing less in mind than the regeneration of the whole human story.

Concretely this worked itself out in the breaking down of the most intractable barriers of the first-century world, between Jews and Gentiles, slaves and free, and even women and men. In the context of our earlier discussion this made the whole world 'home' to those who believed. Ordinary Christians still understand this and are taught it by the eucharist. Attending mass once at Freiburg Cathedral in southern Germany, coffee was served afterwards at the back of the church. One Japanese girl was left out of the general conversation and I discovered that she was in Germany on a two-year study course. I asked her if she was homesick. 'No', she replied, 'the eucharist is my homeland.'

This community which demolishes boundaries is also, naturally, a community of friends, as we learn in John's Gospel:

> You are my friends if you do what I command you. I do not call you servants any longer, because the servant does not know what the master is doing; but I have called you friends, because I have made known to you everything that I have heard from my Father (John 15.14–15).

The early Quakers quite rightly described the Christian community as 'a society of friends'. Friends are free and equal, not divided by authority structures, by class or caste.

Paul's letter to Philemon shows how becoming a Christian cuts across deep-rooted social boundaries. 'I am sending Onesimus back to you ... no longer as a slave but more than a slave, a beloved brother', he writes.

Our meeting at the eucharist to share fellowship as a society of friends challenges us to find political structures to do justice to that reality. The great Swiss theologian Karl Barth used to say that whilst Christianity did not endorse any one political order there was a *nisus* within it, a drive or tendency, towards democracy, that is a society where power is vested in all members of the community. The mistake would be to confuse any of the politics we today call 'democracies' with the 'democracy' of the kingdom, of the society of friends. On the contrary the eucharist should teach us deep dissatisfaction with these democracies. Of course, they give us much for which we have to be thankful, but by the standards of the kingdom they are rudimentary indeed.

As we 'learn Christ' in the education of the eucharistic table are we not called to seek an adequate and nuanced education for all, recognizing and respecting the variety of human ability, and not honouring one type above others? Is what we learn there really compatible with a system which privileges some above others simply because their parents are wealthy? Again, when we take the sharing in our common life seriously, is it not clear that responsibility for 'the commons' – what we now call in an indecent phrase 'the utilities' – should be vested in all? Land, water, energy – these are God's gift to the human race, not given so that a tiny class of managers and politicians can enrich themselves by exploiting them. Managing these resources is a political task for the whole body. From this perspective the abandonment of ideas of common ownership, rooted as these were in the picture of Acts 4, is a sad retreat.

Ideas of common ownership have been abandoned because they seem Utopian, unrealizable in the 'real world'. It is in this context that we turn to the last rooting of our eucharistic practice in the gospel narrative. The fixation with the 'Last' Supper is surely quite extraordinary when we recall that the Gospels tell us it was not the last supper at all, but that Jesus broke bread with the disciples in the resurrection meals. Emmaus is as much a forerunner of the eucharist as the meal in the upper room, if not more so. It is as if the Church found the Risen Lord too much to handle, and was happier contemplating a dead Saviour and singing mournful songs about him instead. But as well as a society of friends we are an Easter people!

In one of the great theological manifestos of this century, written in response to the Jewish Marxist Ernst Bloch, Jürgen Moltmann insisted that hope is the overriding Christian political virtue, and that it is rooted in the resurrection.[5] For the Greeks, hope was an evil from Pandora's box, because it was always likely to leave you disillusioned. This is precisely the standpoint of our political 'realists', who tell us daily that things cannot be different. The resurrection, however, establishes a different law in history: it says that the impossible can become possible, that there is the possibility for what is radically new and radically other. Christians are not bound by Gramsci's motto: 'Pessimism of the intellect, optimism of the will'. According to Paul it was rather, bearing, believing and hoping all things, not to maintain the status quo, but in the process of being carried along by God's long revolution. The meal with the Risen Lord, then, ought to be the seedbed of political imagination and creativity.

The Gospels, said an eighteenth-century biblical scholar, 'breathe resurrection', and they do so because the figure of Jesus does so. In James Joyce's beautiful coinage Jesus is the 'gracehoper' who dreams of a quite different future, which he calls God's kingdom, which he teaches his disciples both to pray and work for. It is the truth of his hoping which is manifest in the resurrection.

On the one side the meal with the Risen Lord is a protest, a critique. It protests against unequal structures in society. It protests against the abuse of the material. It protests against injustice and inhumanity. Its function is then to disturb our complacency, to prevent our accepting injustice and oppression as 'normal', to challenge the view of political 'realism'. It says that the 'realism' of the 'hard facts' is in fact cynicism, a denial of the human. It is then, in the second place, not only a protest but a movement by which we opt out of the class-competitive society, of cynical assumptions about the inevitability of class division or of nuclear weapons. As such it is a deep act of subversion. 'Jesus is the answer' say the slogans, but of course he is not an answer but an insistent question. This is why he did not found a new religion endowed with infallible dogmas, but a movement towards the kingdom of the God he called 'Father'.

How deep the paradox, then, that from the days of the church in Corinth onwards the unity which the eucharist adumbrates through its sharing of one loaf and one cup has been denied. Wine has been withheld from the laity and the eucharist clericalized. Women have usually been refused permission to preside, and in many churches still are. Rich have gone up to receive before the poor. Black have been forbidden to drink from the same cup as white, and high caste from low caste. In every conceivable way human unity has been denied. But the bread of the eucharist is bread which is broken with the dream of a new humanity based on a 'new covenant' in mind. Its sharing looks forward to an equal sharing overcoming all class, caste, racial and sexual divisions: 'We who are many are one body, for we all partake of the one bread' (1 Corinthians 10.17).

The meal with the Risen Lord is a sacramental anticipation of a community in which people live for others; of a society in which each gives according to their abilities to each according to their needs. It does not create a model community, a little group of saved which others may envy. It begins the movement towards the creation of a counter-culture, a culture which will incarnate the values of Christ, the holy jester and divine fool. At the last Passover meal he speaks of his blood poured out for many, for the inclusion of all in God's promises. He dreams therefore of 'one world' under those promises, a dream which Luke translates into story form in his account of the day of Pentecost. The 'Parthians, Medes, Elamites, and residents of Mesopotamia ... and visitors from Rome, both Jews and proselytes, Cretans and Arabs' (Acts 2.9–11) signify for Luke the whole inhabited earth, which now hears of God's promises each in its own tongue. The meal with the Risen Lord is an anticipation of this one human community living at peace.

6

The Eucharist and the Trinity

IN THE PAST twenty years, 'non-realist' views of God have captured the imaginations of many Christians. These views believe that there is no transcendent Other 'out there' to whom we can pray but that God-language is a way of talking of the transcendence of the human project. Others, who do believe in a transcendent Other, believe that this Other is the origin of all things, the mystery of the world, but does not intervene actively in the course of human history. Theologically, arguments for the latter view are weighty and impressive. If God *can* act but does nothing to stop acts of appalling human wickedness, for example, then what kind of being are we dealing with?

I cannot speak for all those who continue to believe in a transcendent Other who acts within history, but can only record my own reasons for doing so. The first is a sense of presence which will not go away no matter how sceptical I try to become. The Welsh poet R. S. Thomas has above all made this sense his own. Some of his poems speak of 'presence' and some of 'absence' but it comes to the same thing. Here is his great poem 'The Presence':

> I pray and incur
> silence. Some take that silence
> for refusal.
>   I feel the power
> that, invisible, catches me

by the sleeve, nudging
   towards the long shelf
that has the book on it I will take down
   and read and find the antidote
to an ailment.
   I know its ways with me;
how it enters my life,
   is present rather
before I perceive it, sunlight quivering
on a bare wall.
   Is it consciousness trying
to get through?
   Am I under
regard?
   It takes me seconds
to focus, by which time
   it has shifted its gaze,
looking a little to one
   side, as though I were not here.

It has the universe
   to be abroad in.
There is nothing I can do
but fill myself with my own
   silence, hoping it will approach
   like a wild creature to drink
there, or perhaps like Narcissus
to linger a moment over its transparent face.[1]

I can speak of my second reason for continuing to believe in
the God who is Other than this creation only in terms of
what the Reformers called the 'self-evidence' of Scripture. I
do not speak of every word and chapter. There is plenty of
material which has been and continues to be damaging,

especially in the underwriting of patriarchy. However, in large parts of Scripture I find myself met by a voice which speaks to the essential concerns of the world in which I live, and which still generates prophetic witness and human hope.

In both these cases it is not a question of reflecting on the world and concluding that without God it does not make sense, but rather an experience of being met, confronted, questioned, challenged, sometimes inspired. I do, however, also find the resolute atheist view more incredible than any theism. Bertrand Russell's view was that we are evolutionary accidents crawling about on a cooling cinder. Every precious relationship and every experience, whether of joy, beauty or tragedy, cries out against this.

And so I continue to pray to, or within the movement of, the God I believe is revealed to us in Scripture, the Triune God. It is this God who is celebrated, as the mystery of the world, in the eucharist.

Many Christians feel baffled by the Trinity, and approach it as if it were some mathematical conundrum only to be solved by the Great Logician at the end of time. As a choirboy I remember vividly saying the Athanasian creed at the beginning of each Lent: 'The Father incomprehensible, the Son incomprehensible, the Spirit incomprehensible'. And of course we added, 'the whole b– thing incomprehensible'. When, many years later, I came across Karl Barth's remark that the triunity of God was the secret of God's beauty, and later still discovered, with so many others, 'Celtic spirituality', childhood bafflement had long been replaced by the sense that the concept of the Trinity was the most illuminating of all Christian teachings.

The doctrine, or as David Jenkins prefers to insist, the 'symbol', arose as a response to Christian experience. Jesus, Paul and all the rest worshipped the God of Israel. Paul, like all the authors of the New Testament, believed that God raised Jesus from the dead, and that this event, profoundly mysterious as it was, threw quite new light on the rabbi of Nazareth. It led Christians to bestow on him, in Paul's words, 'the name above every name'. At the same time, God was encountered within the community's life in a way for which the old word 'Spirit' had to be used. What led to the theological exploration of the first four centuries of Christianity which produced the doctrine was not a love for metaphysical quiddities but the attempt to fathom what had to be said about 'God' if the New Testament were taken seriously as revelation, and if Christian experience were to be understood. Of this exploration, par excellence, it is true that *lex orandi lex credendi est* – the shape of our praying deter- mines the shape of what we believe. In this process the eucharist played a decisive role.

Already by the time of Hippolytus, at the turn of the third century, the structure of the thanksgiving prayer is clearly Trinitarian, as it remains to this day. There are two basic rules of Trinitarian grammar. The first is that 'The works of God outside Godself are undivided.' The second is that we may 'appropriate' different aspects of God's work to each of the three persons. So the first part of the eucharistic prayer offers thanks for the blessings of creation (the 'appropriation' of God the Father); the second for the redemption accomplished in Jesus (the 'appropriation' of God the Son); whilst the final part invokes the Holy Spirit, and prays that she may descend on the Church (sanctifica- tion as the 'appropriation' of the Spirit). The centrality of creation is implicit in the use of material elements like bread and wine; of redemption in the recalling of Christ's interpretation of his own death; of sanctification in the meeting of the Church as the seedbed of the new humanity. The eucharist, which was from the beginning the 'normal' form of worship in the Church (i.e. in the strict sense of being the norm for authentic worship) thus inevitably led to that exploration which we call Trinitarian doctrine.

It is surely no coincidence that when the eucharist became only occasional in many Protestant churches after the Reformation the doctrine of the Trinity quickly came to seem remote and alien, and was written off as a piece of theological sophistry, the most irrelevant of all doctrines to real life, as Kant called it. The exploration was deprived of its roots in the Church's worship and so withered. Where it was preserved it was often with a spirit of the shrug of the shoulders: of course, it's all too difficult for human minds, and much too complex for simple Christians, but we accept it in faith. Conversely there may well be a real connection between the liturgical renewal of the present century and the rebirth of interest in Trinitarian theology of which we are currently the astonished witnesses. This connection may be indicated in at least four fundamental ways.

One of the functions of the symbol of the Trinity is to enable the affirmation that God is involved in history, that God has a history, and that God's history interweaves with ours. This affirmation is opposed to the deist idea of God, who exists but does not want to get involved, or the Neoplatonic God who cannot engage with created reality.

The perception that God's being is itself a history begins from the attempt to take the involvement of God in the cross of Jesus seriously. 'Anyone who really talks of the Trinity talks of the cross of Jesus, and does not speculate in heavenly riddles.'[2] On the cross God suffers and dies. That assertion is at the heart of our faith, and for Christians at the heart of the rationality and justifiability of our world – which is otherwise threatened by the meaninglessness of wickedness, pain and death. The doctrine of the Trinity says that God is 'there' on the cross, but that God also remains the Father to whom Jesus prayed and who suffers the death of the Son. It says further that God's continuing redemptive presence springs from and is related in the closest way to this event. The Spirit is identified as the Spirit of the crucified. But in that case to use the word 'God' is not to speak of a remote First Cause, but to recognize history, passion and suffering *within God*. God is who God is in God's history, and God's history includes the cross and by that token all crosses. This recognition has led to the description of God's life as act or event. Prayer, therefore, is not prayer 'to' God but prayer within a history, an entering into or being caught up in an event. Christian prayer is summed up in the words of the eucharistic offertory round:

> To the Father, through the Son
> Offer we this bread and wine
> Which, through the Spirit blest,
> Becomes love's sign.

Christian prayer is Trinitarian prayer not in being prayer to a 'three-headed God' but in being prayer to the Father, through the Son, in the Spirit. The model of all such prayer is the eucharist. It is thanksgiving to the Father of all things made possible through the self-offering of the Son, and offered in the fellowship of the Spirit in the Church. The eucharist is, then, the school of our praying, leading to prayer which is properly Trinitarian and therefore properly Christian, a fact which is imaged with tremendous power by Rublyev's great icon of the Trinity. Here the three Persons sit at the eucharistic table, the bread and wine before them, the table open to all, to the whole tumult of human history and to all of creation. The artist interprets the Trinity through the wonderful story of the heavenly visitors in Genesis 18. As in Jesus' practice, hospitality – table fellowship – is the site of encounter with God and of blessing. In the background is the oak of Mamre, which is also the tree of the cross – creation and redemption together – the history of Abraham and Sarah standing at the beginning of the narrative of which we too are a part. The three Persons each have their pilgrim staves in their hand. God, says Rublyev, is a journeying God, accompanying human beings on the long road to freedom. On that road God invites us to table, for refreshment for the journey, and that invitation calls us into the prayer which is a participation, a sharing, in the divine relations, in the dance or the journey of God.

It is again partly neglect of this school of prayer which has led to the dichotomy between an abstract deism on the one hand, which prays only to 'Almighty God' and knows nothing of the Son, and an equally abstract pietism on the other which prays only to 'Lord Jesus' to the exclusion of the Father. Since the eighteenth century, Protestantism has balanced uneasily between these alternatives. It is a healthy sign that as we begin to come to terms with and recognize the limitations of the Enlightenment we are able once again to recover a Trinitarian form of prayer.

'God is love': the most fundamental Christian assertion. Augustine's *De Trinitate* is an exploration of this statement. His conclusion is that if you are going to maintain it seriously you must talk about relationship at the heart of reality. The symbol of the Trinity says first that the direction in creation which is deepest and most significant, truly 'ultimate', is glimpsed imperfectly in persons. Persons however do not exist outside relationship. We are as we are in relation. When we say 'person' we do not mean 'individual' but 'being-in-relation', and it is in the conviction that here we have the clue to the ultimate nature of reality that we say that 'God is personal' or speak of 'One God in three persons'. 'In the beginning is the relation' (Martin Buber). This is what is maintained by the Trinitarian symbol. The function of the symbol is to say that we cannot go deeper, beyond or behind this, in the direction of any kind of monism in which 'God' finally absorbs all relation. This Nirvanic vision would deny to persons the ultimate value which we believe to be affirmed in the incarnation.

Some anthropologists have argued, and it seems highly plausible, that our contemporary understanding of 'person' owes a great deal to the doctrines of incarnation and Trinity, this despite the fact that theologians have hedged the term 'person' in Trinitarian discourse with all sorts of caveats. Most would nevertheless agree that the Trinitarian symbol 'declares that it is proper to think of relationships as part of the pattern and dynamic of ultimate reality'.[3] It is true that the symbol does not give us a 'fix' on God so that, in the notorious eighteenth-century phrase, 'Christianity is no longer mysterious.' On the other hand if, as Christian faith affirms, the truth about God is affirmed in this symbol then it is the truth of our world which is affirmed as well. What we are told, and what we signify in the eucharist, is that in truly equal and loving relationships we are corresponding, bringing ourselves into line with, the very heart of reality.

As already noted, the various rules of Trinitarian discourse were ways of exploring the statement 'God is love'. The most prominent of these was that the Three are One, and the One is three. The way in which the Cappadocian Fathers, contemporaries of Augustine, tried to elucidate this has recently been much pursued. They talked of a 'mutual indwelling' of the three persons – imaged in medieval art by three overlapping circles. Our contemporary understanding of the way in which relationships work perhaps helps us to understand this. David Jenkins has put it teasingly by saying that what the doctrine of the Trinity promises us is that 'There is a way of my being me which will come about by my finding my being in you. And this will come about when and as you are you and I am I.'[4]

We can unpack this through the recognition of the way in which we all impinge on others. In most relationships there is some sort of power game going on. I am who I am at the expense of my friend, husband, child being fully themselves. The doctrine of the Trinity, however, thinks of fulfilled relationships in which it is precisely who we are which makes the other most fully themselves. So the Son is who 'he' is because the Father is who 'he' is, and both are what they are because the Spirit is what 'she' is.

The eucharist points towards this reality, holds it before us, to make sure we do not forget it. It is called 'communion' because it is the sacrament of shared relationships. The emphasis is not solely on the 'vertical' communion of the soul with God because both Jesus and writers like the author of 1 John insist that that relationship is impossible without the relationship to my neighbour. 'Communion' is image of God sharing with image of God at my side, realizing the image of God who is community in Godself. The God who is in relation is worshipped through the establishment of more whole and more human relationships in a community without edges whose task is to infect the whole world with the vision of the ultimacy of this pattern of relation. In the kingdom, which for Paul was anticipated in the *ecclesia* ('we have the first fruits . . .') and where the eucharist was a prophetic sign, there could be no Jew nor Greek, no male nor female, no slave nor free but only relations in hope, joy and equality, and ultimately 'in' God. 'It is neither fantastically visionary nor beyond all reason', says David Jenkins, 'to take the risk and the hope of commitment to a vision which speaks of a community and a communion where love fulfils love so that everyone is fully human because everyone is fully human.'[5] The symbol of the Trinity sets us free to hope this, to take love absolutely seriously. Of this hope and love the eucharist is the sacramental sign. In the end is the relation. This is what is proclaimed in the bread-breaking.

A third significance of the doctrine relates to the idea of power. Christianity was born in a world where kings had absolute power, where life and death hung on the nod of their head. Within three centuries the rulers of quite a large part of the world were Christian and the temptation was inevitable to understand God, the world ruler, on their model. We see the embarrassment with the Trinity in the iconography of the high Middle Ages. Sometimes we see the picture of Jesus on the cross, supported behind by God the Father, with a dove somewhere in the picture. Alternatively there is picture of the Father seated on the throne with the Son on his lap, again with a dove somewhere. Only in Rublyev's great fifteenth-century icon do we have a picture of three equal Persons, their pilgrim staves in their hand, gathered round the eucharistic table, with the tree of the cross in the background.

The medieval images are hierarchical but, as the Christian socialists of the last century liked to say, quoting the Athanasian creed, the doctrine of the Trinity speaks of a God 'in whom there is none afore and none after, but one perfect equality'. Politically the image of the Trinity speaks of shared power and the will to share power. It was an image, then, of an abolition of hierarchy in favour of a situation where all were prophets, all filled with the Spirit of God in relation.

As the sacrament which arose from the worship of the Trinitarian God, and whose structure mirrored this threefold relation, the eucharist unconsciously preserved an alternative vision of society. Though it was co-opted by a hierarchical Church, with bishops, priests, deacons and laity in an order of strict submission and obedience, it was the fact that alternatives were represented there which made it such a contentious issue at the Reformation. The 'logic' of the divine love, of which the eucharist is the sign-act, is against all exercise of power from above down, against all sectional uses of power, and constructive of the power of love's solidarity. Because the eucharist is 'love's sign', the sign of that being in relation where love fulfils love, it is the signifying of what society must become and how power must be exercised if it is to come into line with reality, if it is not to be grievously warped and twisted by attempting to go against the grain of the universe as discerned in the crucified Lord.

One of the problems of attributing so much, or as some may want to say, 'reading so much into' the eucharist is that it contradicts our experience of the very ordinary, moderately friendly but also often frankly rather dull services we know Sunday by Sunday. No doubt much of this dullness can be put down to poor preaching and sloppy preparation for the liturgy. On the other hand it is also true that it is, much of the time, much more comfortable to retreat from the depths than to brave them. Our experience constantly confirms the great theme of Eliot's poetry that 'Human kind cannot bear very much reality.' On the other hand the superficial also cloys, even if we long to return to its slavery. Flight from reality and hunger for reality, desire for the bread which perishes and for the true bread, jostle together in our lives and form their pattern.

If we suggest, as Eliot does in the *Four Quartets*, that the function of the eucharist is to bring us into touch with reality we need to be careful to use this word in a sufficiently nuanced way. It is true that 'reality' is the death of children from poverty and disease, and torture of the innocent to defend the interests of Mammon. On this line 'reality' is Auschwitz and we condemn ourselves to triviality if we do not face this. It is equally true, however, both that we cannot bear this reality and also that there is very much more to reality than this. The 'trivial' has its own importance. It is interesting how Jesus' parables return above all to household tasks – sweeping a room, mending an old garment, a thrifty housewife trying to make wineskins last one more year, baking bread, putting out the oil lamps at night, and so on. Jesus did not come preaching a hothouse gospel of the existential depths but mischievously speaks of the depths through and in terms of the trivial and ordinary. The importance he gave to the business of eating is a case in point, and there is surely something of the divine humour in the fact that the sacrament we have been given of the mystery of God's love is a sharing of homoepathic portions of bread and wine!

The eucharist therefore has both aspects of reality. In commemorating a death through torture it brings the tortured to mind. In celebrating the sharing of bread it recalls those who have no bread to share. In being a communion of equals it reminds us of the inequality of most of our brothers and sisters. It reflects on the real world. Its concern is that God's kingdom come and be done 'on earth'.

On the other hand the gospel is not about the importance of being earnest. 'Too much humility is a bore', wrote Bonhoeffer, and so is the idea that 'reality' can be exclusively defined in terms of those extraordinary moments of passion, suffering and insight which intervene here and there in our lives. 'Reality' is both. The Jesus who went to the cross was also the Jesus who laughed and joked with his disciples, who was ironical with his enemies, and who enjoyed playing with children. Jesus was the normal human being only as the one who learned his humanity from the laughter of

Sarah, the amorousness of Ruth, the fatherly passion of David, the common sense of the wise, and the eroticism of the Song of Songs.

The flight from reality which constitutes so much of our experience is at the same time a flight from the mystery of who we ourselves are, who our neighbour is, and why and what the world is. The video culture and cable TV is but the latest and most sophisticated attempt to make this denial of the mystery systematic. The fundamental form of the mystery in our experience is our fellow human being. Sooner or later comes the disconcerting realization that the more deeply we know parent, husband, wife or child the less we know them. If we say that 'God' is a mystery this is not because theological algebra is baffling but because God is 'the most personal being', the root of personhood, that reality which persons have to grow into. The Trinity is a mystery because and as it speaks about what relations and persons really are. The eucharist is the sacrament of that mystery. Here we may legitimately speak of an exploration of 'the holy mysteries', which are ultimately relationships.

'God became human', said Luther, 'so that from proud and inhuman gods he might make real human beings.' The eucharist is given to be part of this process; in it we rehearse the question of what it means to become human. We rehearse the mystery of which Jesus, as human being, as being in relation to Martha, Mary, Peter, Judas – is the sign. Because at its ultimate depth the mystery is relation, the sign is naturally 'communion', sharing. It is education for growth, for changing and changing often. It is an invitation to exploration, to perceiving and realizing the mystery which awaits us at every turn of mystery's creation. It is the sacrament of the beauty, depth and mystery of the trivial and ordinary. It is the foretaste and celebration of the resurrection of the flesh.

NOTES

Chapter 1

1. *The Letters of the Younger Pliny* (tr. B. Radice, Penguin, 1963), page 294.
2. Tertullian, *Apology*, chapter 7.
3. Texts in *Early Christian Writings* (tr. M. Staniforth, Penguin, 1968).
4. Justin Martyr, *First Apology*, chapter 57.
5. Augustine, *Letter 138*.
6. Augustine, *City of God*, 10.6.
7. J. Oman, *Grace and Personality* (CUP, 1960), page 189.
8. K. Rahner, *Theological Investigations*, volume 14 (Darton, Longman and Todd, 1976), page 161f.
9. P. Tillich, *Systematic Theology*, volume 2 (James Nisbet, 1968), pages 130–1.
10. G. von Rad, *Old Testament Theology*, volume 2 (SCM, 1962), page 342.

Chapter 2

1. J. L. Segundo, *The Liberation of Theology* (New York, Orbis, 1976), page 43.

Chapter 3

1. C. Myers, *Binding the Strong Man* (New York, Orbis, 1988), pages 205f.
2. Myers, *Binding the Strong Man*, page 206.
3. Irenaeus, *Adversus Haereses*, 4.18.4.
4. A. Thein Durning, *How Much Is Enough?* (Earthscan, 1992), page 51.
5. K. Watkins, *The Oxfam Poverty Report* (Oxfam, 1995).
6. *Our Common Future* (OUP, 1987), page 71.
7. G. and V. Curzon, cited in H. Singer and J. Ansari, *Rich and Poor Countries*, 4th edn (Unwin Hyman, 1988), page 74.

8. B. Coote, *The Trade Trap* (Oxfam, 1992), page 120.
9. C. Elliott, *Comfortable Compassion* (Hodder and Stoughton, 1987), referring to work by R. Prebisch and H. Singer.
10. Singer and Ansari, *Rich and Poor Countries*, page 251.
11. F. Gaffikin and A. Nickson, *Jobs Crisis and the Multinationals* (Birmingham Trade Union Group Publications, no date), page 49.
12. R. J. Barnet, *The Lean Years* (Abacus, 1981), page 171.
13. Cited in S. George, *A Fate Worse than Debt* (Penguin, 1988), page 234.
14. Watkins, *The Oxfam Poverty Report*, page 3.
15. W. Berry, *Home Economics* (San Francisco, Northpoint Press, 1987), pages 56–64.
16. C. Myers, *Who Will Roll Away the Stone?* (New York, Orbis, 1994), pages 166–7.
17. K. Nielsen, 'Global Justice, Capitalism and the Third World' in R. Attfield and B. Wilkins, eds., *International Justice and the Third World* (Routledge, 1992), page 33.
18. For the following points see U. Duchrow, *Alternatives to Global Captialism, Drawn from Biblical History, Designed for Political Action* (The Hague, International Books, 1995).

Chapter 4

1. *The Weekday Missal* (Collins, 1982), page xx.
2. Justin Martyr, *Dialogue with Trypho*, 117.
3. R. Williams, *Eucharistic Sacrifice: The Roots of a Metaphor* (Grove Books, 1982), page 27.
4. Cyprian, *Letter 63*.
5. J. Jeremias, *The Eucharistic Words of Jesus* (SCM, 1966), pages 138f.
6. Augustine, *Sermon 278*.
7. Jeremias, *Eucharistic Words*, pages 230f.
8. R. Girard, *Things Hidden Since the Foundation of the World* (tr. S. Bann and M. Metteer, Athlone Press, 1987), page 225.
9. Jeremias, *Eucharistic Words*, page 255.

CHAPTER 5

1. *Odyssey*, 23 (tr. W. Shewring, Worlds Classics, 1980).
2. J. Bowlby, *Attachment and Loss* (Penguin, 1969), page 353.
3. It was not true for Karen Silkwood in the United States, or Hilda Murrell in Britain, either, and we do not know how representative their deaths are. See J. Cook, *Red Alert* (New English Library, 1986), pages 237f.
4. T. Balasuriyea, *The Eucharist and Human Liberation* (SCM, 1979), page 21.
5. J. Moltmann, *The Theology of Hope* (SCM, 1966).

CHAPTER 6

1. R. S. Thomas, 'The Presence' in *Later Poems* (Macmillan, 1984).
2. J. Moltmann, *The Crucified God* (SCM, 1974), page 207.
3. D. Jenkins, *The Contradiction of Christianity* (SCM, 1976), page 155.
4. Jenkins, *Contradiction of Christianity*, page 158.
5. Jenkins, *Contradiction of Christianity*, page 145.

FURTHER READING

ON THE EUCHARIST

N. Lash, *His Presence in the World* (Sheed and Ward, 1980).
J. Greenhalgh and E. Russell, eds., *Signs of Faith, Hope and Love* (St Mary's, Bourne St., 1987).

ON POLITICS AND COMMUNITY

T. Cullinan, *The Passion of Political Love* (Sheed and Ward, 1987).
J. Reader, *Local Theology* (SPCK, 1994).

ON THE ECONOMY

C. Myers, *Who Will Roll Away the Stone?* (New York, Orbis, 1994).
T. Gorringe, *Capital and the Kingdom* (SPCK, 1994).
U. Duchrow, *Alternatives to Global Capitalism* (International Books, 1995).

ON THE TRIUNE GOD

D. Jenkins, *The Contradiction of Christianity* (SCM, 1976).
J. Moltmann, *History and the Triune God* (SCM, 1991).

INDEX

Index

von Rad, G. 14, 88
Rahner, K. 12, 88
real presence 9
Rublyev 80, 84f
Russell, B. 77

sacraments 10ff
sacrifice 51ff
Schoenberg, A. 62
Segundo, J. 88
Semprun, J. 5
sermons 69
sexuality 26ff
signs 4ff
Silkwood, K. 90
symbols 13

Tertullian 2, 88
Thein Durning, A. 88
Tillich, P. 13, 88
Third World 36
Thomas, R. S. 75
Torres, C. 43
Trajan 1
transignification 9ff
transubstantiation 4, 10, 49
Trinity 77ff
Troeltsch, E. 69

Watkins, K. 88
Wilde, O. 68
Williams, R. 47, 89

SCRIPTURE REFERENCES